Bread and Wine

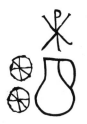

Bread and Wine

Readings for Lent and Easter

PLOUGH PUBLISHING HOUSE

Published by Plough Publishing House
Walden, New York
Robertsbridge, England
Elsmore, Australia
www.plough.com

Copyright © 2003 by Plough Publishing House
All Rights Reserved

22 21 20   13 12 11 10 9
ISBN 10: 0-87486-926-9
ISBN 13: 978-0-87486-926-2

A catalog record for this book is available from the British Library.
Library of Congress Cataloging-in-Publication Data

Bread and wine : readings for Lent and Easter.
    p. cm.
Includes bibliographical references and index.
  ISBN 0-87486-926-9 (alk. paper)
  1. Lent—Prayer-books and devotions—English. 2. Devotional
calendars.
  BV85 .B663 2003
  242'.34—dc21

                                    2002012679

Printed in the USA

Looking at Stars

The God of curved space, the dry
God, is not going to help us, but the son
whose blood splattered
the hem of his mother's robe.

JANE KENYON

Because Lent begins on a different date each year, the readings in this book are arranged by number, not date. The first 46 readings cover the season of Lent proper, beginning on Ash Wednesday and ending on Holy Saturday. The last two sections of the book offer additional readings on the themes of resurrection and new life.

Contents

Introduction

You can't conceive, my child, nor can I or anyone, the appalling
strangeness of the mercy of God. **GRAHAM GREENE**

DOROTHY SAYERS writes that to make the Easter
story into something that neither startles, shocks, terri-
fies, nor excites is "to crucify the Son of God afresh."
Certainly that would have been unthinkable for Jesus'
first followers, who experienced it firsthand: the heady
excitement of his entry into Jerusalem, the traitorous
cunning of Judas and the guilty recognition of their
own cowardice, the terror of his slow suffocation, and
finally the disarming wonder of an empty grave and a
living body resurrected from the dead.

As for us, his latter-day disciples, few would deny
the magnitude or drama of these events. But how many
of us embrace their pain and promise? How many of

us, even at Easter, give Christ's death and resurrection any more attention than the weather?

To observe Lent is to strike at the root of such complacency. Lent (literally "springtime") is a time of preparation, a time to return to the desert where Jesus spent forty trying days readying for his ministry. He allowed himself to be tested, and if we are serious about following him, we will do the same.

First popularized in the fourth century, Lent is traditionally associated with penitence, fasting, alms-giving, and prayer. It is a time for "giving things up" balanced by "giving to" those in need. Yet whatever else it may be, Lent should never be morose – an annual ordeal during which we begrudgingly forgo a handful of pleasures. Instead, we ought to approach Lent as an opportunity, not a requirement. After all, it is meant to be the church's springtime, a time when, out of the darkness of sin's winter, a repentant, empow-ered people emerges. No wonder one liturgy refers to it as "this joyful season."

Put another way, Lent is the season in which we ought to be surprised by joy. Our self-sacrifices serve no purpose unless, by laying aside this or that desire, we are able to focus on our heart's deepest longing:

unity with Christ. In him—in his suffering and death, his resurrection and triumph—we find our truest joy.

Such joy is costly, however. It arises from the horror of our sin, which crucified Christ. This is why Meister Eckhart points out that those who have the hardest time with Lent are "the good people." Most of us are willing to give up a thing or two; we may also admit our need for renewal. But to *die* with Christ?

Spiritual masters often refer to a kind of "dread," the nagging sense that we have missed something important and have been somehow untrue—to ourselves, to others, to God. Lent is a good time to confront the source of that feeling. It is a time to let go of excuses for failings and shortcomings; a time to stop hanging on to whatever shreds of goodness we perceive in ourselves; a time to ask God to show us what we really look like. Finally, it is a time to face up to the personal role each of us plays in prolonging Christ's agony at Golgotha. As Richard John Neuhaus (paraphrasing John Donne) advises, "Send not to know by whom the nails were driven; they were driven by you, by me."

And yet our need for repentance cannot erase the good news that Christ overcame all sin. His resurrection frees us from ourselves. His empty tomb turns our attention away from all that is wrong with us and with the world, and spurs us on to experience the abundant life he promises.

"Christ must increase, and I must decrease," the apostle John declares, and his words resonate through the readings collected in this book. The men and women who wrote them faced the same challenge we do: to discover Christ – the scarred God, the weak and wretched God, the crucified, dying God of blood and despair – amid the alluring gods of our feel-good age. He reveals the appalling strangeness of divine mercy, and the Love from which it springs. Such Love could not stay imprisoned in a cold tomb. Nor need we, if we truly surrender our lives to it.

The Editors
August 2002

Invitation

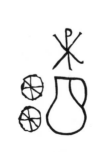

THE BALLAD OF READING GAOL

Oscar Wilde

…And thus we rust Life's iron chain
    Degraded and alone:
And some men curse, and some men weep,
    And some men make no moan:
But God's eternal Laws are kind
    And break the heart of stone.

And every human heart that breaks,
    In prison-cell or yard,
Is as that broken box that gave
    Its treasure to the Lord,
And filled the unclean leper's house
    With the scent of costliest nard.

Ah! happy those whose hearts can break
    And peace of pardon win!
How else may man make straight his plan
    And cleanse his soul from Sin?
How else but through a broken heart
    May Lord Christ enter in?

1

My Messy House

Kathleen Norris

WHEN I'M WORKING as an artist-in-residence at parochial schools, I like to read the psalms out loud to inspire the students, who are usually not aware that the snippets they sing at Mass are among the greatest poems in the world. But I have found that when I have asked children to write their own psalms, their poems often have an emotional directness that is similar to that of the biblical psalter. They know what it's like to be small in a world designed for big people, to feel lost and abandoned. Children are frequently astonished to discover that the psalmists so freely express the more unacceptable emotions, sadness and even anger, even anger at God, and that all of this is in the Bible that they hear read in church on Sunday morning.

Children who are picked on by their big brothers and sisters can be remarkably adept when it comes to writing cursing psalms, and I believe that the writing process offers them a safe haven in which to work through their desires for vengeance in a healthy way. Once a little boy wrote a poem called "The Monster Who Was Sorry." He began by admitting that he hates it when his father yells at him: his response in the poem is to throw his sister down the stairs, and then to wreck his room, and finally to wreck the whole town. The poem concludes: "Then I sit in my messy house and say to myself, 'I shouldn't have done all that.'"

"My messy house" says it all: with more honesty than most adults could have mustered, the boy made a metaphor for himself that admitted the depth of his rage and also gave him a way out. If that boy had been a novice in the fourth-century monastic desert, his elders might have told him that he was well on the way toward repentance, not such a monster after all, but only human. If the house is messy, they might have said, why not clean it up, why not make it into a place where God might wish to dwell?

2

Repent

William Willimon

John the Baptizer appeared in the wilderness, preaching a baptism of repentance... **MARK 1:4**

THE CHURCH OF TODAY lives in an ethically debilitating climate. Where did we go wrong? Was it the urbane self-centeredness of Peale's *Power of Positive Thinking* and its therapeutic successors? Was it the liberal, civic-club mentality of the heirs to the Social Gospel? Now we waver between evangelical TV triumphalism with its Madison Avenue values or live-and-let-live pluralism which urges open-mindedness as the supreme virtue. And so a recent series of radio sermons on "The Protestant Hour" urged us to "Be Good to Yourself." This was followed by an even more innocuous series on "Christianity as Conflict Management." Whatever the gospel means, we tell ourselves, it could not mean death. Love, divine or human, could never exact something so costly. After all, our culture is at least vestigially Christian and isn't that enough?

The first week of Lent begins with old John the Baptist. His sermons could not be entitled, "Be Good to Yourself." This prophetic "voice crying in the wilderness" appears "preaching a baptism of repentance for the forgiveness of sins" (Mark 1:4). He is not the Christ. John is the one who gets us ready. How does one prepare for this new age? Repent, change your ways, and get washed.

Like the prophets of old, John's word strikes abrasively against the easy certainties of the religious Establishment. He will let us take no comfort in our rites, tradition, or ancestry. Everybody must submit to be made over. Everybody must descend into the waters, especially the religiously secure and the morally sophisticated. God is able to raise up children even from stones if the Chosen fail to turn and repent.

How shocked was the church to see its Lord appear on the banks of the Jordan asking John to wash him too (Matt. 3:14–15). How can it be that the Holy One of

God should be rubbing shoulders with naked sinners on their way into the waters? The church struggled with this truth. Why must our Lord be in this repenting bath?

When Jesus was baptized, his baptism was not only the inauguration of his mission, but also a revelation of the shockingly unexpected nature of his mission. His baptism becomes a vignette of his own ministry. Why so shocking? On two occasions, Jesus uses "baptism" to refer to his own impending *death*. He asks his half-hearted disciples, "Can you drink the cup that I must drink, or be baptized with the baptism with which I must be baptized?" (Mark 10:38).

As he submits to John's bath of repentance, Jesus shows the radical way he will confront the sin that enslaves humanity. Jesus' "baptism," begun in the Jordan and completed on Golgotha, is repentance, self-denial, *metanoia* to the fullest. John presents his baptism as a washing from sin, a turning from self to God. Jesus seeks even more radical *metanoia*.

His message is not the simple one of the Baptist, "Be clean." Jesus' word is more painful – "Be killed." The washing of this prophetic baptism is not cheap. "You also must consider yourselves dead," Paul tells the Romans (Rom. 6:11). In baptism, the "old Adam" is drowned. "For you have died, and your life is hid with Christ in God" (Col. 3:3).

To be baptized "into Christ" and "in the name of Christ" means to be incorporated into the way of life which characterized his life, the life of the empty one, the servant, the humble one, the obedient one, obedient even unto death (Phil. 2:6–11).

That day at the Jordan, knee deep in cold water, with old John drenching him, the Anointed One began his journey down the *via crucis*. His baptism intimated where he would finally end. His whole life was caught up in this single sign. Our baptism does the same.

The chief biblical analogy for baptism is not the water that washes but the flood that drowns. Discipleship is more than turning over a new leaf. It is more fitful and disorderly than gradual moral formation. Nothing less than daily, often painful, lifelong death will do. So Paul seems to know not whether to call what happened to him on the Damascus Road "birth" or "death" – it felt like both at the same time.

In all this I hear the simple assertion that we must submit to change if we would be formed into this cruciform faith. We may come singing "Just as I Am," but we will not stay by being our same old selves. The needs of the world are too great, the suffering and pain too extensive, the lures of the world too seductive for us to begin to change the world unless we are changed, unless conversion of life and morals becomes our pattern. The status quo is too alluring. It is the air we breathe, the food we eat, the six-thirty news, our institutions, theologies, and politics. The only way we shall break its hold on us is to be transferred to another dominion, to be cut loose from our old certainties, to be thrust under the flood and then pulled forth fresh and newborn. Baptism takes us there.

On the bank of some dark river, as we are thrust backward, onlookers will remark, "They could kill somebody like that." To which old John might say, "Good, you're finally catching on."

3

In Mirrors

Walter Wangerin

IN MIRRORS I SEE MYSELF. But in mirrors made of glass and silver I never see the *whole* of myself. I see the me I want to see, and I ignore the rest.

Mirrors that hide nothing hurt me. They reveal an ugliness I'd rather deny. Yow! Avoid these mirrors of veracity!

My wife is such a mirror. When I have sinned against her, my sin appears in the suffering of her face. Her tears reflect with terrible accuracy my selfishness. My *self!* But I hate the sight, and the same selfishness I see now makes me look away.

"Stop crying!" I command, as though the mirror were at fault. Or else I just leave the room. Walk away.

Oh, what a coward I am, and what a fool! Only when I have the courage fully to look, clearly to know myself—even the evil of myself—will I admit my need for healing. But if I look away from her whom I have hurt, I have also turned away from her who might forgive me. I reject the very source of my healing.

My denial of my sin protects, preserves, perpetuates that sin! Ugliness in me, while I live in illusions, can only grow the uglier.

Mirrors that hide nothing hurt me. But this is the hurt of purging and precious renewal—and these are the mirrors of dangerous grace.

The passion of Christ, his suffering and his death, is such a mirror. Are the tears of my dear wife hard to look at? Well, the pain in the face of Jesus is harder. It is my *self* in my extremest truth. My sinful self. The death he died reflects a selfishness so extreme that by it I was divorced from God and life and light completely: I raised my *self* higher than God! But because the Lord God is the only true God, my pride did no more, in the end, than to condemn this false god of my *self* to death. For God will *be* God, and all the false gods will fall before him.

So that's what I see reflected in the mirror of Christ's crucifixion: my death. My rightful punishment. My sin and its just consequence. Me. And precisely because it is so accurate, the sight is nearly intolerable.

Nevertheless I will not avoid this mirror! No, I will carefully rehearse, again this year, the passion of my Jesus—with courage, with clarity and faith; for this is the mirror of dangerous grace, purging more purely than any other.

For this one is not made of glass and silver, nor of fallen flesh only. This mirror is made of righteous flesh and of divinity, both—and this one loves me absolutely. My wife did not choose to take my sin and so to reflect my truth to me. She was driven, poor woman. But Jesus did choose—not only to take the sin within himself, not only to reflect the squalid truth of my personal need, but also to reveal the tremendous truth of his grace and forgiveness. He took that sin *away*.

This mirror is not passive only, showing what is; it is active, creating new things to be. It shows me a new me behind the shadow of a sinner. For when I gaze at his crucifixion, I see my death indeed—but my death *done!*

His death is the death of the selfish one, whom I called ugly and hated to look upon.

And resurrection is another me.

4

Living Lent

Barbara Cawthorne Crafton

WE DIDN'T EVEN KNOW what moderation was. What it felt like. We didn't just work: we inhaled our jobs, sucked them in, *became* them. Stayed late, brought work home—it was never enough, though, no matter how much time we put in.

We didn't just smoke: we lit up a cigarette, only to realize that we already had one going in the ashtray.

We ordered things we didn't need from the shiny catalogs that came to our houses: we ordered three times as much as we could use, and then we ordered three times as much as our children could use.

We didn't just eat: we stuffed ourselves. We had gained only three pounds since the previous year, we told ourselves. Three pounds is not a lot. We had gained about that much in each of the twenty-five years since high school. We did not do the math.

We redid living rooms in which the furniture was not worn out. We threw away clothing that was merely out of style. We drank wine when the label on our prescription said it was dangerous to use alcohol while taking this medication. "They always put that on the label," we told our children when they asked about this. We saw that they were worried. We knew it was because they loved us and needed us. How innocent they were. We hastened to reassure them: "It doesn't really hurt if you're careful."

We felt that it was important to be good to ourselves, and that this meant that it was dangerous to tell ourselves no. About anything, ever. Repression of one's desires was an unhealthy thing. *I work hard,* we told ourselves. *I deserve a little treat.* We treated ourselves every day.

And if it was dangerous for us to want and not have, it was even more so for our children. They must never know what it is to want something and not have it immediately. It will make them bitter, we told ourselves. So we anticipated their needs and desires.

We got them both the doll and the bike. If their grades were good, we got them their own telephones.

There were times, coming into the house from work or waking early when all was quiet, when we felt uneasy about the sense of entitlement that characterized all our days. When we wondered if fevered overwork and excess of appetite were not two sides of the same coin—or rather, two poles between which we madly slalomed. *Probably yes*, we decided at these times. Suddenly we saw it all clearly: *I am driven by my creatures—my schedule, my work, my possessions, my hungers. I do not drive them; they drive me. Probably yes. Certainly yes. This is how it is.* We arose and did twenty sit-ups. The next day the moment had passed; we did none.

After moments like that, we were awash in self-contempt. *You are weak. Self-indulgent. You are spineless about work and about everything else. You set no limits. You will become ineffective.* We bridled at that last bit, drew ourselves up to our full heights, insisted defensively on our competence, on the respect we were due because of all our hard work. We looked for others whose lives were similarly overstuffed; we found them. "This is just the way it is," we said to one another on the train, in the restaurant. "This is modern life. Maybe some people have time to measure things out by teaspoonfuls." Our voices dripped contempt for those people who had such time. We felt oddly defensive, though no one had accused us of anything. *But not me. Not anyone who has a life. I have a life. I work hard. I play hard.*

When did the collision between our appetites and the needs of our souls happen? Was there a heart attack? Did we get laid off from work, one of the thousands certified as extraneous? Did a beloved child become a bored stranger, a marriage fall silent and cold? Or, by some exquisite working of God's grace, did we just find the courage to look the truth in the eye and, for once, not blink? How did we come to know that we were dying a slow and unacknowledged death? And that the only way back to life was to set all our packages down and begin again, carrying with us only what we really needed?

We travail. We are heavy laden. Refresh us, O homeless, jobless, possession-less Savior. You came naked, and naked you go. And so it is for us. So it is for all of us.

5

A Look Inside

Edna Hong

The grinding power of the plain words of the Gospel story is like the power of millstones; and those who can read them simply enough will feel as if rocks had been rolled upon them.

G. K. CHESTERTON

"DID YOU EVER LOOK inside yourself and see what you are not?" the crippled daughter in one of Flannery O'Connor's short stories shouts at her spiritually crippled mother. Few of us have looked long enough into ourselves to see that what seems to us and to others as normally attractive is actually as graceless as a scarecrow and even repulsive. It is an easy matter for the physical eye to spot physical deformity and blemishes in others and in oneself. It is not so easy for the eye of the spirit to spot a spiritual dwarf, hunchback, or cripple, although it is easier to see these spiritual deformities in others than in oneself.

This x-ray look at others is called "naked truth," "unvarnished truth." In literature and art it is called realism. But to spot it in one's self is not only difficult but painful, and no one wants to take the descending path to that naked, unvarnished truth, with all its unacceptable humiliations. It is much more comfortable to stay on the level of the plain and ordinary, to go on being just plain and ordinary. Yet it is to this path that Lent invites us.

The reason Lent is so long is that this path to the truth of oneself is long and snagged with thorns, and at the very end one stands alone before the broken body crowned with thorns upon the cross. All alone—with not one illusion or self-delusion to prop one up. Yet not alone, for the Spirit of Holiness, who is also the Spirit of Helpfulness, is beside you and me. Indeed, this Spirit has helped to maneuver you and me down that dark, steep path to this crucial spot.

"But I've been to that place before," the born-again Christian may protest. "Of course, the non-Christian and perhaps the brought-up Christian need to be brought to that crucial spot, but of all people, we who are born again should not. Is it not a kind of heresy to say that we need to go there again and again and again? Is it not to doubt our salvation, the power of our Savior to deliver us from the dominion of darkness?"

Lent would indeed be a futile liturgical farce if the redeemed were henceforth sinless and if the tides of human nature were not always moving even the twice-born, who have not shed their human nature, in the direction of complacency and taking it all for granted. The tides of God always move in exactly the opposite direction—toward an ever deeper skepticism about ourselves (that we may have all the more confidence in God), toward an ever deeper self-distrust (that we may trust in God all the more). The high tides of human nature, even of the twice-born, move to drown the conscience. As long as the consciences of the born-again are housed in human flesh and bone, they are prone to the sleep of death and need continual rescuing.

Our self-indulgent and self-flattering age looks upon the self-maltreating and self-hating practices of the monastic and desert ascetics as pathetic and futile. We shiver to think of Suso making himself a cross with thirty protruding nails and wearing it on his back like a porcupine skin day and night. We laugh to think of him never taking a bath in order to mortify his comfort-seeking body. But for us who feel the need for daily showers (because soap has not broken dirt's dominion), it most certainly is not spiritual self-mortification and asceticism that convince us we no longer need spiritual shower baths. It is rather our comfort-seeking spirits.

But the spirit of truth does not seek comfort. The purpose of Lent is not to escape the conscience, but to create a healthy hatred for evil, a heartfelt contrition for sin, and a passionately felt need for grace. This continuous movement of faith from a sense of sin to grace and forgiveness ends only when the spirit is ultimately released.

ROBERT HERRICK, a 17th-century poet, wrote these striking lines in "To Keep a True Lent."

> Is this a Fast, to keep
> the larder lean?
> And clean
> From fat of veals and sheep?
> Is it to quit the dish
> of flesh, yet still
> To fill

The platter high with fish?
Is it to fast an hour,
   Or ragg'd to go,
     Or show
A down-cast look and sour?
No: 'tis a Fast to dole
   Thy sheaf of wheat
     And meat
With the hungry soul.
It is to fast from strife
   And old debate,
     And hate;
To circumcise thy life.
To show a heart grief-rent;
   To starve thy sin,
     Not bin;
And that's to keep thy Lent.

Robert Herrick was moving the keeping of Lent in the right direction, away from mortifications of the flesh – fasting, hair shirts, pebbles in the shoes, burrs next to the skin, dour faces, and all that. But he stopped somewhat short of the true purpose of Lent, which is not to starve one's sin but to get rid of it. And then – *then* comes the spiritual energy, spiritual activity, spiritual eloquence…

Edna Hong · 23

These do not come from ecstasy but from a humbly grateful heart. Forgiveness of sins is what the gospel is all about. Forgiveness of sins is what Christ's death upon the cross is all about. The purpose of Lent is to arouse. To arouse the sense of sin. To arouse a sense of guilt for sin. To arouse the humble contrition for the guilt of sin that makes forgiveness possible. To arouse the sense of gratitude for the forgiveness of sins. To arouse or to motivate the works of love and the work for justice that one does out of gratitude for the forgiveness of one's sins.

To say it again—this time, backward: There is no motivation for works of love without a sense of gratitude, no sense of gratitude without forgiveness, no forgiveness without contrition, no contrition without a sense of guilt, no sense of guilt without a sense of sin.

In other words, a guilty suffering spirit is more open to grace than an apathetic or smug soul. Therefore, an age without a sense of sin, in which people are not even sorry for not being sorry for their sins, is in rather a serious predicament. Likewise an age with a Christianity so eager to forgive that it denies the need for forgiveness. For such an age, therefore, Lent can scarcely be too long!

"I have found only one religion that dares to go down with me into the depth of myself," wrote G. K. Chesterton. And it is true. No other religion dares to take me *down* to the new beginning. Hence Lent is not a tediously long brooding over sin. Lent is a journey that could be called an upward descent, but I prefer to call it a downward ascent. It ends before the cross, where we stand in the white light of a new beginning. So fresh and new, says Chesterton, waxing lyrical, "that one can be grey and gouty – but only five minutes old!" The spirit that shuns this downward ascent all its livelong days eventually ends up an aged fetus. There is an infinite difference between being brand-new and five minutes old and being an aged fetus!

6

Surrender Is Everything

Jean-Pierre de Caussade

During the days of Jesus' life on earth, he offered up prayers and petitions with loud cries and tears to the one who could save him from death, and he was heard because of his reverent submission.

HEBREWS 5:7

SURRENDER OF THE HEART to God includes every possible way of obedience to God, because it means giving up one's very being to God's good pleasure. Since this surrender is effected by unalloyed love, it includes in its embrace every kind of operation his good pleasure may bring to pass. Thus at every moment we practice a surrender that has no limits, a surrender that includes all possible methods and degrees of service to God. It is not our business to decide what the ultimate purpose of such submission may be, but our sole duty is to submit ourselves to all that God sends us and to stand ready to do his will at all times.

What God requires of the soul is the essence of self-surrender. The free gifts he asks from us are self-denial, obedience and love. The rest is his business. It does not matter whether the soul is carefully fulfilling the duties of one's state in life, or quietly following the leadings it is given, or submitting peacefully to the dealings of grace either to the body or to the soul. In all this, the soul is exercising within the one overall act of self-surrender. It is not a matter of single, isolated incidents or the duty of one moment, but the act always carries with it the full merit and good effect which a sincere will always has, although the outcome does not depend on the single act of surrender. What the soul desires to do is done as in the sight of God.

If it happens that God's will sets a limit to the exercise of some particular faculty of ours, he sets no limit on our wills. The good pleasure of God, God's being and essence are the object of the will, and through the exercise of love it is united with God without limit, manner or measure. If this love results in the exercise of only one faculty or another for a certain object, this means that the will of God goes only so far, it contracts itself, so to speak, restricting itself to the specific needs of the moment, engaging the faculties and then going on into the heart. Finding the heart pure, untrammeled and holding nothing back, he communicates his will fully to it, because his love has given it an infinite capacity by emptying it of all created things and making it capable of union with God.

O heavenly purity! O blessed emptying! O unreserved submission! Through you God is welcomed into the very center of the heart! It matters not what my abilities may be then, provided that I possess you, Lord. Do what you will with this insignificant creature. Whether it be that I should work, or become inspired, or be the recipient of your impressions, it is all the same. Everything is yours, everything is from you and for you. I no longer have anything to be concerned about, anything to do. I have no hand in the arrangement of one single moment of my life; everything belongs to you. I do not need to add or subtract anything, nor to seek after or mull over anything. It is for you, Lord, to regulate everything: direction, humiliations, sanctification, perfection and salvation—all are your business, Lord. Mine is to be satisfied with your work and not to demand the choice of action or condition, but to leave everything to your good pleasure.

7

The Relinquished Life

Oswald Chambers

So it is ourselves that we must spread under Christ's feet, not coats or lifeless branches or shoots of trees, matter which wastes away and delights the eye only for a few brief hours. But we have clothed ourselves with Christ's grace, with the whole Christ – "for as many of you as were baptized into Christ have put on Christ" – so let us spread ourselves like coats under his feet.

ANDREW OF CRETE

NO ONE IS EVER UNITED with Jesus Christ until he is willing to relinquish not sin only, but his whole way of looking at things. To be born from above of the Spirit of God means that we must let go before we lay hold, and in the first stages it is the relinquishing of all pretense. What our Lord wants us to present to him is not goodness, nor honesty, nor endeavor, but real, solid sin; that is all he can take from us. And what does he give in exchange for our sin? Real, solid righteousness. But we must relinquish all pretense of being anything, all claim of being worthy of God's consideration.

Then the Spirit of God will show us what further there is to relinquish. There will have to be the relinquishing of my claim to my right to myself in every phase. Am I willing to relinquish my hold on all I possess, my hold on my affections, and on everything, and to be identified with the death of Jesus Christ?

There is always a sharp, painful disillusionment to go through before we do relinquish. When one really sees himself as the Lord sees him, it is not the abominable sins of the flesh that shock him, but the awful nature of the pride of his own heart against Jesus Christ. When he sees himself in the light of the Lord, the shame and the horror and the desperate conviction come home. If you are up against the question of relinquishing, go through the crisis, relinquish all, and God will make you fit for all He requires of you.

The imperative need spiritually is to sign the death warrant of the disposition of sin, to turn all emotional impressions and intellectual beliefs into a moral verdict against the disposition of sin, *viz,* my claim to my right to myself. Paul says, "I have been crucified with Christ"; he does not say, "I have determined to imitate Jesus Christ" or, "I will endeavor to follow Him" but, "I have been *identified* with Him in His death." When I come to such a moral decision and act upon it, then all that Christ wrought *for* me on the Cross is wrought *in* me. The free committal of myself to God gives the Holy Spirit the chance to impart to me the holiness of Jesus Christ.

CO-CRUCIFIXION. Have I made this decision about sin—that it must be killed right out in me? It takes a long time to come to a moral decision about sin, but it is the great moment in my life when I do decide that just as Jesus Christ died for the sin of the world, so sin must die out in me, not to be curbed or suppressed or counteracted, but crucified. No one can bring anyone else to this decision. We may be earnestly convinced, and religiously convinced, but what we need to do is to come to the decision once and for all.

Haul yourself up, take a time alone with God, make the moral decision and say, "Lord, identify me with your death until I know that sin is dead in me."

Make the moral decision that sin in you must be put to death.

Ask yourself: Am I prepared to let the Spirit of God search me until I know what the disposition of sin is – the thing that lusts against the Spirit of God in me? If so, will I agree with God's verdict on that disposition of sin – that it should be identified with the death of Jesus? I cannot reckon myself "dead indeed unto sin" unless I have been through this radical issue of will before God.

Have I entered into the glorious privilege of being crucified with Christ until all that is left is the life of Christ in my flesh and blood? "I have been crucified with Christ and I no longer live, but Christ lives in me" (Gal. 2:20).

These words mean the breaking of my own independence with my own hand and surrendering to the supremacy of the Lord Jesus. No one can do this for me, I must do it myself. God may bring me up to the point three hundred and sixty-five times a year, but he cannot put me through it. It means breaking the husk of my individual independence of God, and the emancipating of my personality into oneness with himself, not for my own ideas, but for absolute loyalty to Jesus. There is no possibility of dispute when once I am there. Very few of us know anything about loyalty to Christ – *"For My sake."* It is that which makes the iron saint.

Has that break come? All the rest is pious fraud. The one point to decide is: Will I give up, will I surrender to Jesus Christ, and make no conditions whatever as to how the break comes? I must be broken from my self-realization, and immediately that point is reached, the reality of the supernatural identification takes place at once, and the witness of the Spirit of God is unmistakable.

It is not just a question of giving up sin, but of giving up my natural independence and self-assertiveness, and this is where the battle has to be fought. It is the things that are right and noble and good from the natural standpoint that keep us back from God's best. To discern that natural virtues antagonize surrender to God is to bring our soul into the center of its greatest battle. Very few of us debate with the sordid and evil and wrong, but we do debate with the good. It is the good that hates the best, and the higher up you get in the scale of the natural virtues, the more intense is the opposition to Jesus Christ. "They that are Christ's have crucified the flesh" (Gal. 5:24). It is going to cost the natural in you everything, not something. Jesus said, "If anyone would come after me, he must deny *himself*," and a person has to realize who Jesus Christ is before he will do it. Beware of refusing to go to the funeral of your own independence.

8

The Royal Road

Thomas à Kempis

If we do not bear the cross of the Master, we will have to bear the cross of the world, with all its earthly goods. Which cross have you taken up? Pause and consider. **SADHU SUNDAR SINGH**

THERE WILL ALWAYS be many who love Christ's heavenly kingdom, but few who will bear his cross. Jesus has many who desire consolation, but few who care for adversity. He finds many to share his table, but few who will join him in fasting. Many are eager to be happy with him; few wish to suffer anything for him. Many will follow him as far as the breaking of bread, but few will remain to drink from his passion. Many are awed by his miracles, few accept the shame of his cross.

Many love Christ as long as they encounter no hardship; many praise and bless him as long as they receive some comfort from him. But if Jesus hides himself and leaves them for a while, they either start complaining or become dejected. Those, on the contrary, who love him for his own sake and not for any comfort of their own, praise him both in trial and anguish of heart as well as in the bliss of consolation. Even if Jesus should never comfort them, they would continue to praise and thank him. What power there is in a pure love for Jesus—love that is free from all self-interest and self-love!

Do not those who always seek consolation deserve to be called mercenaries? Do not those who always contemplate their own profit and gain prove that they love themselves rather than Christ? Where can we find anyone who is willing to serve God for nothing? It is surely rare to find a person spiritual enough to strip himself of all earthly things. And where can we find anyone so truly poor in spirit that he is free from being dependent on created things? Such a person is worth far more than the jewels brought from the most distant lands.

If one were to give all his wealth, it is nothing. If he were to try and make amends for all his sins, it is worth little. If he excelled in learning and knowledge, he is still far afield. If he had great virtue and much ardent devotion, he still would lack a great deal, and especially the one thing that is most necessary to him. What is this one thing? He must give up everything, especially himself, retaining no private store of selfish desires. Then, when he has done all that he knows ought to be done, let him consider it as nothing. He should not bask in any applause he may receive, but consider himself an ordinary servant. As it says in the Gospel, "When you have done everything you were told to do, you should say, 'I am an unworthy servant; I have only done my duty'" (Luke 17:10).

Many find the command, "Deny thyself, take up your cross and follow Me" (Matt. 16:24) too hard. But it will be much harder to hear that final word: "Depart from me, you who are cursed, into the everlasting fire" (Matt. 25:41). Those who hear the word of the cross and follow it willingly now, need not fear judgment. This sign of the cross will be in the heavens when the Lord comes to judge. Then everyone who serves the cross, who in this life made themselves one with the Crucified, will draw near with confidence to Christ, the judge.

Why, then, do you fear to take up the cross when through it you can win the kingdom? There is no salvation or hope of everlasting life but in the cross.

Take up your cross, therefore, and follow Jesus, and you will inherit everlasting life. Behold, in the cross is everything, and upon your dying on the cross everything depends. There is no other way to life and to true inward peace than the way and discipline of the cross. Go where you will, seek what you want, you will not find a higher way, nor a less exalted but safer way, than the way of the cross. Arrange and order everything to suit your desires and you will still have to bear some kind of suffering, willingly or unwillingly.

There is no escaping the cross. Either you will experience physical hardship or tribulation of spirit in your soul. At times you will be forsaken by God, at times troubled by those about you and, what is worse, you will often grow weary of yourself. You cannot escape, you cannot be relieved by any remedy or comfort but must bear with it as long as God wills. For he wishes you to learn to bear trial without consolation, to submit yourself wholly to him that you may become more humble through suffering. No one understands the passion of

Christ so thoroughly or heartily as the one who has suffered similarly.

The cross, therefore, is unavoidable. It waits for you everywhere. No matter where you may go, you cannot escape it, for wherever you go you take yourself along. Turn where you will—above, below, without, or within—you will find the cross.

If you willingly carry the cross, it will carry you. It will take you to where suffering comes to an end, a place other than here. If you carry it unwillingly, you create a burden for yourself and increase the load, though still you have to bear it. If you try to do away with one cross, you will find another and perhaps a heavier one. How do you expect to escape what no one else can avoid? Which saint was exempt? Not even Jesus Christ was spared. Why is it that you look for another way other than the royal way of the holy cross?

The whole life of Christ was a cross. And the more spiritual progress you strive for, the heavier will your crosses become, for as your love for God increases so will the pain of your exile.

When you willingly carry your cross, every pang of tribulation is changed into hope of solace from God. Besides, with every affliction the spirit is strengthened by grace. For it is the grace of Christ, and not our own virtue, that gives us the power to overcome the flesh and the world. You will not even fear your enemy, the devil, if you arm yourself with faith and are signed with the cross of Christ.

Decide then, like a good and faithful servant of Christ, to bear bravely the cross of your Lord. It was out of love that he was crucified for you. Drink freely from the Lord's cup if you wish to be his friend. Leave your need for consolation to God. Let him do as he wills. On your part, be ready to bear sufferings and consider how in these sufferings lies your greatest consolation. The sufferings of this life are not worthy to be compared with the glory to come.

When you get to the point where for Christ's sake suffering becomes sweet, consider yourself fortunate, for you have found paradise on earth. But as long as adversity irks you, as long as you try to avoid suffering, you will be discontent and ill at ease.

Realize that to know Christ you must lead a dying life. The more you die to yourself, the more you will live unto God. You will never enjoy heavenly things unless you are ready to suffer hardship for Christ. Nothing is more acceptable to God, nothing more helpful for you on this earth. When there is a choice to be made, take the narrow way. This alone will make you more like Christ.

9

To Know the Cross

Thomas Merton

I pray that we may be found worthy to be cursed, censured, and ground down, and even put to death in the name of Jesus Christ, so long as Christ himself is not put to death in us.

PAULINUS OF NOLA

THE CHRISTIAN must not only accept suffering: he must make it holy. Nothing so easily becomes unholy as suffering.

Merely accepted, suffering does nothing for our souls except, perhaps, to harden them. Endurance alone is no consecration. True asceticism is not a mere cult of fortitude. We can deny ourselves rigorously for the wrong reason and end up by pleasing ourselves mightily with our self-denial.

Suffering is consecrated to God by faith – not by faith in suffering, but by faith in God. Some of us believe in the power and the value of suffering. But such a belief is an illusion. Suffering has no power and no value of its own.

It is valuable only as a test of faith. What if our faith fails the test? Is it good to suffer, then? What if we enter into suffering with a strong faith in suffering, and then discover that suffering destroys us?

To believe in suffering is pride: but to suffer, believing in God, is humility. For pride may tell us that we are strong enough to suffer, that suffering is good for us because we are good. Humility tells us that suffering is an evil which we must always expect to find in our lives because of the evil that is in ourselves. But faith also knows that the mercy of God is given to those who seek him in suffering, and that by his grace we can overcome evil with good. Suffering, then, becomes good by accident, by the good that it enables us to receive more abundantly from the mercy of God. It does not make us good by itself, but it enables us to make ourselves better than we are. Thus, what we consecrate to God in suffering is not our suffering but our selves.

Only the sufferings of Christ are valuable in the sight of God, who hates evil, and to him they are valuable chiefly as a sign. The death of Jesus on the cross has an infinite meaning and value not because it is a death, but because it is the death of the Son of God. The cross of Christ says nothing of the power of suffering or of death. It speaks only of the power of him who overcame both suffering and death by rising from the grave.

The wounds that evil stamped upon the flesh of Christ are to be worshiped as holy not because they are wounds, but because they are *his* wounds. Nor would we worship them if he had merely died of them, without rising again. For Jesus is not merely someone who once loved us enough to die for us. His love for us is the infinite love of God, which is stronger than all evil and cannot be touched by death.

Suffering, therefore, can only be consecrated to God by one who believes that Jesus is not dead. And it is of the very essence of Christianity to face suffering and death not because they are good, not because they have meaning, but because the resurrection of Jesus has robbed them of their meaning.

TO KNOW THE CROSS is not merely to know our own sufferings. For the cross is the sign of salvation, and no one is saved by his own sufferings. To know the cross is to know that we are saved by the sufferings of Christ; more, it is to know the love of Christ who underwent suffering and death in order to save us. It is, then, to know Christ. For to know his love is not merely to know the story of his love, but to experience in our spirit that we are loved by him, and that in his love the Father manifests his own love for us, through his Spirit poured forth into our hearts...

The effect of suffering upon us depends on what we love. If we love only ourselves, suffering is merely hateful. It has to be avoided at all costs. It brings out all the evil that is in us, so that the one who loves only himself will commit any sin and inflict any evil on others merely in order to avoid suffering himself.

Worse, if a person loves himself and learns that suffering is unavoidable, he may even come to take a perverse pleasure in suffering itself, showing that he loves and hates himself at the same time.

In any case, if we love ourselves, suffering inexorably brings out selfishness, and then, after making known what we are, drives us to make ourselves even worse than we are.

If we love others and suffer for them, even without a supernatural love for other people in God, suffering can give us a certain nobility and goodness. It brings out something fine in our natures, and gives glory to God who made us greater than suffering. But in the end a natural unselfishness cannot prevent suffering from destroying us along with all we love.

If we love God and love others in him, we will be glad to let suffering destroy anything in us that God is pleased to let it destroy, because we know that all it destroys is unimportant. We will prefer to let the accidental trash of life be consumed by suffering in order that his glory may come out clean in everything we do.

If we love God, suffering does not matter. Christ in us, his love, his Passion in us: that is what we care about. Pain does not cease to be pain, but we can be glad of it because it enables Christ to suffer in us and give glory to his Father by being greater, in our hearts, than suffering would ever be.

10

Discipleship and the Cross

Dietrich Bonhoeffer

Jesus began to teach them that the Son of Man must suffer many things and be rejected by the elders, chief priests and teachers of the law, and that he must be killed and after three days rise again. He spoke plainly about this, and Peter took him aside and began to rebuke him.

But when Jesus turned and looked at his disciples, he rebuked Peter. "Out of my sight, Satan!" he said. "You do not have in mind the things of God, but the things of men."

Then he called the crowd to him along with his disciples and said: "If anyone would come after me, he must deny himself and take up his cross and follow me." **MARK 8:31–34**

SUFFERING AND REJECTION are the summary expression of Jesus' cross. Death on the cross means to suffer and to die as someone rejected and expelled. That it is Peter, the rock of the church, who incurs guilt here immediately after his own confession to Jesus Christ and after his appointment by Jesus, means that from its very inception the church itself has taken offense at the suffering Christ. It neither wants such a Lord nor does it, as the Church of Christ, want its Lord to force upon it the law of suffering.

This makes it necessary for Jesus to relate clearly and unequivocally to his own disciples the "must" of suffering. Just as Christ is Christ only in suffering and rejection, so also they are his disciples only in suffering and rejection, in being crucified along with Christ. Discipleship as commitment to the person of Jesus Christ places the disciple under the law of Christ, that is, under the cross.

"If anyone would come after me, he must deny himself." Just as Peter, in denying Christ, said, "I do not know the man," so also should each disciple say this to herself or himself. Self-denial can never be defined as some profusion—be it ever so great—of individual acts of self-torment or of asceticism. It is not suicide, since there, too, a person's self-will can yet assert itself. Self-denial means knowing only Christ, and no longer oneself. It means seeing only Christ, who goes ahead of us, and no longer the path that is too difficult for us. Again, self-denial is saying only: He goes ahead of us; hold fast to him.

The cross is not adversity, nor the harshness of fate, but suffering coming solely from our commitment to Jesus Christ. The suffering of the cross is not fortuitous, but necessary. The cross is not the suffering tied to natural existence, but the suffering tied to being Christians. The cross is never simply a matter of suffering, but a matter of suffering *and* rejection, and even, strictly speaking, rejection for the sake of Jesus Christ, not for the sake of some other arbitrary behavior or confession. The cross always simultaneously means rejection, and that the disgrace of suffering is part of the cross. Being expelled, despised, and abandoned by people in one's suffering, as we find in the unending lament of the psalmist, is an essential feature of the suffering of the cross, yet one no longer comprehensible to a form of Christian life unable to distinguish between bourgeois and Christian existence.

The first suffering we must experience is the call sundering our ties to this world. This is the death of the old human being in the encounter with Jesus Christ.

Whoever enters discipleship enters Jesus' death, and puts his or her own life into death; this has been so from the beginning. The cross is not the horrible end of a pious, happy life, but stands rather at the beginning of community with Jesus Christ. Every call of Christ leads to death. Whether with the first disciples we leave home and occupation in order to follow him, or whether with Luther we leave the monastery to enter a secular profession, in either case, the one death awaits us, namely, death in Jesus Christ, the dying away of our old form of being human in Jesus' call.

But there is yet another suffering and yet another disgrace that no Christian escapes. Only Christ's own suffering is the suffering of reconciliation. Yet because Christ did suffer for the sake of the world's sins, because the entire burden of sin fell upon him, and because Jesus Christ bequeaths to the disciples the fruit of his suffering—because of all this, temptation and sin also fall upon the disciples. It covers them with pure shame, and expels them from the gates of the city like the scapegoat. Thus does the Christian come to bear sin and guilt for others.

Individual Christians would collapse under the weight of this, were they not themselves borne by him who bore all sins. In this way, however, they can, in the power of Christ's own suffering, overcome all the sins that fall upon them by forgiving them. Thus do Christians become the bearers of burdens: "Bear one another's burdens, and in this way you will fulfill the law of Christ" (Gal. 6:2). Just as Christ bears our burdens, so also are we to bear the burdens of our brothers and sisters. The law of Christ which must be fulfilled is the bearing of the cross. The burden of my brother or sister that I am to bear is not only that person's external fate, that person's character and personality, but is in a very real sense that person's sin. I cannot bear it except by forgiving it, in the power of the cross of Christ in which I, too, have a portion.

Those who are not prepared to take up the cross, those who are not prepared to give their life to suffering and rejection by others, lose community with Christ, and are not disciples. Discipleship is commitment to the suffering Christ.

WHETHER WE REALLY have found God's peace will be shown by how we deal with the sufferings that will come upon us. There are many Christians who do, indeed, kneel before the cross of Jesus Christ, and yet reject and struggle against every tribulation in their own lives. They believe they love the cross of Christ, and yet they hate that cross in their own lives. And so in truth they hate the cross of Jesus Christ as well, and in truth despise that cross and try by any means possible to escape it.

Those who acknowledge that they view suffering and tribulation in their own lives only as something hostile and evil can see from this very fact that they have not at all found peace with God. They have basically merely sought peace with the world, believing possibly that by means of the cross of Jesus Christ they might best come to terms with themselves and with all their questions, and thus find inner peace of the soul. They have used the cross, but not loved it. They have sought peace for their own sake. But when tribulation comes, that peace quickly flees them. It was not peace with God, for they hated the tribulation God sends.

Thus those who merely hate tribulation, renunciation, distress, defamation, imprisonment in their own lives, no matter how grandiosely they may otherwise speak about the cross, these people in reality hate the cross of Jesus and have not found peace with God. But those who love the cross of Jesus Christ, those who have genuinely found peace in it, now begin to love even the tribulations in their lives, and ultimately will be able to say with scripture, "We also boast in our sufferings."

11

Followers, Not Admirers

Søren Kierkegaard

IT IS WELL KNOWN that Christ consistently used the expression "follower." He never asks for admirers, worshippers, or adherents. No, he calls disciples. It is not adherents of a teaching but followers of a life Christ is looking for.

Christ understood that being a "disciple" was in innermost and deepest harmony with what he said about himself. Christ claimed to *be* the way and the truth and the life (Jn. 14:6). For this reason, he could never be satisfied with adherents who accepted his teaching—especially with those who in their lives ignored it or let things take their usual course. His whole life on earth, from beginning to end, was destined solely to have followers and to make admirers impossible.

Christ came into the world with the purpose of saving, not instructing it. At the same time—as is implied in his saving work—he came to be *the pattern*, to leave footprints for the person who would join him, who would become a follower. This is why Christ was born and lived and died in lowliness. It is absolutely impossible for anyone to sneak away from the Pattern with excuse and evasion on the basis that it, after all, possessed earthly and worldly advantages that he did not have. In that sense, to admire Christ is the false invention of a later age, aided by the presumption of "loftiness." No, there is absolutely nothing to admire in Jesus, unless you want to admire poverty, misery, and contempt.

What then, is the difference between an admirer and a follower? A follower is or strives to be what he admires. An admirer, however, keeps himself personally detached. He fails to see that what is admired involves a claim upon him, and thus he fails to be or strive to be what he admires.

To want to admire instead of to follow Christ is not necessarily an invention by bad people. No, it is more an invention by those who spinelessly keep themselves detached, who keep themselves at a safe distance.

Admirers are related to the admired only through the excitement of the imagination. To them he is like an actor on the stage except that, this being real life, the effect he produces is somewhat stronger. But for their part, admirers make the same demands that are made in the theater: to sit safe and calm. Admirers are only too willing to serve Christ as long as proper caution is exercised, lest one personally come in contact with danger. They refuse to accept that Christ's life is a demand. In actual fact, they are offended by him. His radical, bizarre character so offends them that when they honestly see Christ for who he is, they are no longer able to experience the tranquillity they so much seek after. They know full well that to associate with him too closely amounts to being up for examination. Even though he says nothing against them personally, they know that his life tacitly judges theirs.

And Christ's life indeed makes it manifest, terrifyingly manifest, what dreadful untruth it is to admire the truth instead of following it. When there is no danger, when there is a dead calm, when everything is favorable to our Christianity, then it is all too easy to confuse an admirer with a follower. And this can happen very quietly. The admirer can be under the delusion that the position he takes is the true one, when all he is doing is playing it safe. Give heed, therefore, to the call of discipleship!

If you have any knowledge at all of human nature, who can doubt that Judas was an admirer of Christ! And we know that Christ at the beginning of his work had many admirers. Judas was precisely such an admirer and thus later became a traitor. It is not hard to imagine that those who only admire the truth will, when danger appears, become traitors. The admirer is infatuated with the false security of greatness; but if there is any inconvenience or trouble, he pulls back. Admiring the truth, instead of following it, is just as dubious a fire as the fire of erotic love, which at the turn of the hand can be changed into exactly the opposite, to hate, jealousy, and revenge.

There is a story of yet another admirer—Nicodemus. Despite the risk to his reputation, despite the effort on his part, Nicodemus was only an admirer; he never became a follower. It is as if he might have said to Christ, "If we are able to reach a compromise, you and I, then I will accept your teaching in eternity. But here in this world, no, I cannot. Could you not make an exception for me? Would it not be enough if once in a while, at great risk to myself, I come to you during the night, but during the day (yes, I confess it, I feel how humiliating this is for me and how disgraceful, indeed also how very insulting it is toward you) I say 'I do not know you'?" See in what a web of untruth an admirer can entangle himself!

Nicodemus, I am quite sure, was well-meaning. I'm also sure he was ready in the strongest phrases to attest that he accepted the truth of Christ's teaching. Yet, is it not true that the more strongly someone makes assurances, while his life still remains unchanged, the more he is only making a fool of himself? If Christ had permitted a cheaper edition of follower—an admirer who swears by all that is high and holy that he is convinced—then Nicodemus might very well have been accepted. But he was not!

Now suppose that there is no longer any special danger, as it no doubt is in so many of our Christian countries, bound up with publicly confessing Christ. Suppose there is no longer need to journey in the night. The difference between following and admiring still remains. Forget about danger connected with confessing Christ and think rather of the real danger which is inescapably bound up with being a Christian. Does not the

Way – Christ's requirement to die to the world and deny self – does this not contain enough danger?

The admirer never makes any true sacrifices. He always plays it safe. Though in word he is inexhaustible about how highly he prizes Christ, he renounces nothing, will not reconstruct his life, and will not let his life express what it is he supposedly admires. Not so for the follower. No, no. The follower aspires with all his strength to be what he admires. And then, remarkably enough, even though he is living amongst a "Christian people," he incurs the same peril as he did when it was dangerous to openly confess Christ. And because of the follower's life, it will become evident who the admirers are, for the admirers will become agitated with him. Even these words will disturb many – but then they must likewise belong to the admirers.

12

The Center

J. Heinrich Arnold

One who does not seek the cross of Jesus isn't seeking the glory of Christ. **ST. JOHN OF THE CROSS**

EVERY BELIEVER KNOWS that Christ went the way of the cross for our sakes. But it is not enough just to *know* this. Each of us must find the cross. He suffered in vain unless we are willing to die for him as he died for us. Christ's way was a bitter way. It ended in a victory of light and life, but it began in the feeding trough of an animal in a cold stable, and passed through tremendous need: through suffering, denial, betrayal, and finally, complete devastation and death on a cross. If we call ourselves his followers, we must be willing to take the same path.

When a grain of wheat is laid in the earth, it dies. It no longer remains a grain, but through death it brings forth fruit. This is the way of true Christianity. It is the way Jesus went when he died on the cross for each of us. If we want our lives to be fruits of Christ's death on the cross, we cannot remain individual grains. We must be ready to die too.

Christ died on the cross to break the curse of evil and vanquish it once and for all. If we do not believe in the power of evil, we cannot comprehend this. Until we realize that the main reason for his coming to earth was to do this on our behalf—to free us from the powers of darkness—we will never fully understand our need for the cross. We can search the whole world, but we will find forgiveness of sins and freedom from torment nowhere except at the cross.

Many people say, "God is so great, so mighty, that he could have saved humankind without the cross." But that is not true. We should remember that God is not only one hundred percent love—which might have allowed him to forgive our sins without the cross. He is also one hundred percent justice. To kill the son of God was the most evil deed ever done. But it was just through that deed that God showed his greatest love and gave everyone the possibility of finding peace with him.

The image of a sweet, gentle Savior, like the thought of an all-loving God, is wonderful, but it is only a small part of the picture. It insulates us from the real power of his touch. Christ comforts and heals, saves and forgives – we know that; but we must not forget that he judges too. If we truly love him, we will love *everything* in him; not only his compassion and mercy, but his sharpness too. It is his sharpness that prunes and purifies.

There is something in modern thinking which rebels against the Atonement. Perhaps our idea of an all-loving God keeps us from wanting to face judgment. We think that love and forgiveness is all that is needed, yet that is not the whole Gospel – it makes God too human.

Christ's love is not the soft love of human emotion, but a burning fire that cleanses and sears. It is a love that demands self-sacrifice. My father writes:

The Earth can be conquered in no other way than through sacrifice. Satan can be vanquished in no other way than through the Lamb. Jesus is the sacrifice who, being perfect, has been victorious over evil. In the sacrificial love of a lamb, Jesus has overcome the dragon, disarmed Satan and smashed his weapons on the cross. Thus it is impossible for Satan to prevail with his instruments of darkness and death against anyone who is one in faith with the crucified Christ.

Here we see that if Christ's freedom is to become ours, we must be one with the *crucified* Christ. His cross is the center, the linchpin, of the struggle between God and Satan, and as such it must become the center of our hearts too. In the cross alone is victory! In the cross alone is purity! It is there that the hosts of evil are overcome; that Christ's love to each human being springs eternal and gives us peace.

Unless these truths live in our hearts—unless they grip us in a deeply personal way and infuse our very being—they remain nothing but meaningless words. Jesus offers to give himself to each one of us—by inviting us to eat his flesh and drink his blood. Jesus does not offer a philosophy, but life. He is real food. He will change *everything* for someone who experiences this, not only for that moment but for all eternity.

When we know Jesus in the depths of our hearts, we will begin to realize (even if only to a tiny degree) what he went through for our sake. This means surrendering ourselves to him in prayer and quiet, confessing our sins to one another, and laying them before the cross in a spirit of repentance. Then he will accept us and give us reconciliation with God, a clean conscience, and a pure heart. In rescuing us from inner death and granting us new life, his love for us will spill over into our own hearts and give us a great love for him.

Naturally it cannot end here, however. The experience of personal purification at the cross is vital, yet to remain focused on that alone would be useless. Christ's love is so great, it must lift our minds above our little struggles—and any preoccupation with our own salvation—so that we can see the needs of others, and beyond that the greatness of God and his Creation. The cross is so much greater than the personal; it has cosmic significance, for its power embraces the whole earth and more than this earth!

There are secrets that only God knows, and the crucifixion at Golgotha is perhaps the greatest of them all. Paul speaks of its mystery and says only that it pleased

God to let his full nature dwell in Jesus and to reconcile to himself everything on earth and in heaven "through the shedding of his blood on the cross" (Col. 1:19–20). At the cross, then, not only earth but also heaven and all the powers and principalities of the angel world will be reconciled to God. Certainly not we, and maybe not even the angels, will ever fully understand this. But one thing we know: Christ overcame death, the last enemy, and through this, something took place that continues to have power far beyond the limits of our planet.

Temptation

LACHRIMAE AMANTIS

Geoffrey Hill

What is there in my heart that you should sue
so fiercely for its love? What kind of care
brings you as though a stranger to my door
through the long night and in the icy dew

seeking the heart that will not harbor you,
that keeps itself religiously secure?
At this dark solstice filled with frost and fire
your passion's ancient wounds must bleed anew.

So many nights the angel of my house
has fed such urgent comfort through a dream,
whispered "your lord is coming, he is close"

that I have drowsed half-faithful for a time
bathed in pure tones of promise and remorse:
"tomorrow I shall wake to welcome him."

13

Keeping Watch

Philip Berrigan

May he not come suddenly and find you sleeping. What I say to you, I say to all: "Watch!" **MARK 13:36–37**

I AM PONDERING the passage at Mark 13:36, and my thoughts return to the winter of 1943, to a nineteen-year-old draftee at Camp Gordon, now Fort Gordon, Georgia. The old Springfield rifle is heavy, the Georgia winters are damp and cold and dark and–Lord, Gawd!–I've gotta walk guard for four hours.

And do I ever watch! I watch for the officer of the guard. If he hears a weak challenge ("Halt! Who goes there?") or finds me forgetful of the password (Geronimo) or hiding or smoking, it's weekend KP for a month. The minutes and hours drag agonizingly by. I'm cold to the bone. Do I ever watch for six in the morning and the dawn!

So, in this way, the military forced "watching" on me. I didn't choose it. But "watching" should be voluntary, should be a nonviolent way of life. Scripture is full of it:

Yes, like the eyes of a servant on the hand of his master. Like the eyes of a maid on the hand of her mistress. So our eyes are on the Lord our God till we are shown favor.
Psalm 123:2

My soul looks for the Lord more than sentinels for daybreak. More than sentinels for daybreak let Israel look for the Lord. *Psalm 130:6*

Therefore, stay awake! For you do not know on which day your Lord will come. *Matthew 24:42*

Be sure of this: If the master of the house had known the hour when the thief was coming, he would not have let his house be broken into. *Luke 12:39*

Jesus warns us against "sleeping," against being out of it while the world lurches on in its mindless, violent way. Jesus summons us to regard the world as Gethsemane, to watch and stay awake. Three times he had to awaken

Peter, James, and John in the garden as he suffered their abandonment when they slept and later their abandonment in his time of greatest need.

Psychological studies reveal that Americans live in less than forty percent awareness, as though our minds and spirits cringe before the banality and ugliness of national life. Such studies imply an enormous waste of potential lost to trivial pursuits—game-playing, fantasizing, daydreaming, television, self-pity, brooding, boredom, gluttony in food or drink. Lost is the prospect of personal and social renewal, reading, study, meditation, prayer, teaching, service to the poor, justice and peacemaking, and nonviolent resistance to power-mongering government and corporations. The scripture likens such crippled attentiveness to death—death before one dies.

Yes, Jesus commands us to wake and watch. Watch for who or what? Watch for the Holy Spirit of God who teaches us the life of Jesus Christ. The Holy Spirit continues the ministry and sacrifice of Jesus, consecrating people unto Him:

> The Holy Spirit will teach you everything and remind you of all that I told you.   *John 14:26*

Upon request, the Holy Spirit will shower us with gifts that help us to become like Christ: wisdom, understanding, knowledge, counsel, piety, fear of God, fortitude. Upon request, the Holy Spirit will give us the faith necessary to control our fear. "I believe, God; help my unbelief." Upon request, the Holy Spirit will speak the word of God to our hearts, the word of truth and life.

Watch the words of others, since God often speaks to us through sisters and brothers. Watch for conformity between words and deeds, and when the two are the same, watch only their deeds. Watch for heroic women and men who give their lives tending victims – the bombed, starved, raped, tortured – and to exposing the victimizers from within prison and without. Watch the hope that they give you by the speech of their lives, and then dare to extend hope to others.

Watch the world through nonviolence and become a student of systemic evil. Watch nuclearism and the blind, venal paranoia of the nuclear club. Watch tens upon tens of wars going on worldwide and the arms sales of the United States, Russia, and Britain feeding those wars. Watch refugees in Yugoslavia, central Africa, Cambodia, and Bosnia. Watch the transnational money system that undergirds corporations. Watch corporations themselves as they declare themselves "stateless," as they automate, downsize, fire workers, pay less and less taxes, and punish the ecology.

Yes, watch corporations and their accountability to one thing: a financial system rightly called a global gambling casino. Watch them as they boast about "statelessness" while investing vast sums in lobbyists and "buyable" politicians. Watch how the biggest and the best–General Motors, Lockheed Martin, Boeing, McDonnell Douglas, General Dynamics, Raytheon, and Hughes Aircraft–combine military and economic oppression. Watch the corporations as they scorn government after having obtained everything they need: the collapse of Communism, tariff and trade agreements, deregulation, lower taxes, less trouble from unions, lower wages, police and military protection.

Only one weapon remains against such massive organizations of greed, luxury, and exploitation: direct nonviolent action. When official deceit and betrayal become intolerable, when national life becomes more ugly and despairing, perhaps Americans will regain their faith in God and will again say "No!" to the political charlatans, nuclear warriors, and corporate parasites. Their "No!" will take them to the streets and the official hellholes to expose and withstand the legality of terrorism and tyranny.

Watch, learn, act—the formula for a faithful and sane life.

14

The Common Criminal

Fleming Rutledge

WHEN JOHN THE BAPTIST was languishing in prison, he sent a message to Jesus asking him to explain himself. Apparently John could not understand why Jesus had not begun to exercise his Messianic authority and power in the way that John thought he would. Jesus replied with a definition of his ministry and then said, "Blessed is he who takes no offense at me" (Matthew 11:6). Yet, we are repeatedly told throughout the four Gospels, people did just that. Here is the story of two women who took offense at him.

The first woman (let's call her Sally) told me she was having trouble finding an Episcopal church that she liked. I suggested that she try St. Such and Such.

"Oh, no," she exclaimed. "I could never go there." "Why not?" I asked. To my amazement she said, "I would have to look at that big cross they have behind the altar with that figure of Christ hanging on it. It would upset me terribly!"

The second woman (let's call her Jane) is a woman whose husband and children I used to know pretty well. Although Jane appeared to be a very agreeable person to those who saw her socially at the club or the church, I knew it to be a fact that she made life difficult for her family. She was manipulative, domineering, willful, and unforgiving. The fact that she had a pleasing personality on the surface just made it worse, because she was used to getting her own way with blandishments. It was almost impossible to get hold of her to help her see what she was doing; she considered herself a person of superior virtue.

During Holy Week several years ago she said something that, from my point of view, was deeply revealing. First I should explain that, although many churches have been doing dramatic readings of the Passion narrative for many years, the church she belonged to had not done it before. On one Palm Sunday, she participated in such a dramatized version for the first time. As a member of the congregation, representing the crowd, she was supposed to shout, "Let him be crucified!" This part of the reading is often a significant moment for those who take part; in fact, I know people whose faith has been kindled, or rekindled, at that moment. After the service was over, several of us were standing around at the coffee hour talking about how moving the service had been. People were especially talking about how they had felt when they shouted, "Let him be crucified!" At this point Jane said, with considerable energy, "I just couldn't do it! I just couldn't say it! I just couldn't say such an awful thing!"

I have often thought, since, how terribly sad that was. In her stubborn blindness, Jane could not identify herself as a sinner like all the rest of us. She could not admit that she, too, was capable of evil thoughts and malicious deeds. She was preoccupied with her own virtue and her own religiousness. Because of this, she could not see who Jesus is or who she is. A wise Benedictine monk once said, "If you can't handle the violence in the Psalms, you can't come to terms with the violence in yourself." This is even more true of the cross. If we can't look at the cross, then we can't look at ourselves either.

I have one more little story to tell. This is another story about Sally, the woman who didn't want to look at the figure of Jesus on the crucifix. She told some of her friends about an experience she'd had in a department store. In order to appreciate this, you have to picture the department store and you have to picture Sally. The store in question is fashionable and elegant. Sally herself is fashionable and elegant, the epitome of aristocratic dignity. She bought an expensive blouse at the store and took it with her in a shopping bag. Unfortunately, the saleswoman had forgotten to remove the white plastic device that was attached to the blouse. When Sally tried to go through the door, the alarms went off and the security forces pounced upon her. "Oh, my dear, how horrible for you!" cried her friends, listening to the story, "It must have been so distressing! Did you call your husband? Did you have your identification? Did you call your lawyer? Did you ask to see the president of the store?"

"Oh," said Sally, "that wasn't a problem. I didn't have any trouble establishing who I was. That wasn't the bad part. The really bad part was the feeling of being treated like a common criminal!"

Those were her exact words. Like a common criminal. This is the woman who won't go to the church in her neighborhood because it has a figure of Jesus on the cross and she doesn't want to look at it.

Sally was able to tell the department store who she was; and yet the truth is that she does not know who she is. I tried to explain to Sally that the feeling of shame she had felt was a clue to the meaning of the death of Jesus, who was arrested like a common criminal, exhibited to the public like a common criminal, executed like a common criminal. I was unable to put this across. She does not believe herself to be guilty of anything. Wronged, yes; misunderstood, yes; undervalued, yes; imperfect, perhaps; but not guilty, certainly not sinful. Because she believes herself to be one of the "good" people, because she could never, never commit a small sin like shoplifting, she cannot see the connection between Jesus' death as a common criminal and herself.

Sally could not hear the message of Good Friday, Jane could not hear it, but perhaps you can hear it today, on their behalf as well as your own. When you reflect upon Jesus Christ hanging on the cross of shame, you understand the depth and weight of human sin.

How do we measure the size of a fire? By the number of firefighters and fire engines sent to fight against it. How do we measure the seriousness of a medical condition? By the amount of risk the doctors take in prescribing dangerous antibiotics or surgical procedures. How do we measure the gravity of sin and the incomparable vastness of God's love for us? By looking at the magnitude of what God has done for us in Jesus, who *became like a common criminal* for our sake and in our place.

When you really come to know the unconditional love and forgiveness of Jesus, then you will also come to know the depth of your own participation in sin. *And at the very same moment* (this is the glory of Good Friday) you will come to know the true reality, the true joy and gladness, of the good news of salvation in Jesus Christ our Lord.

15

The Divine Scandal

Emil Brunner

But we preach Christ crucified: a stumbling block to Jews and foolishness to the Gentiles. **I CORINTHIANS 1:23**

WHY IS IT THAT PAUL describes the gospel as a folly and a scandal and that worldly wisdom feels so repelled by it?

The wisdom of this world gives us occasion to be proud of our own achievement. Even the Jewish religion with its piety holds that it is still we who must do the decisive thing in order to win the good pleasure of God. This applies still more to oriental and mystical religions. The latter do not mortify human nature nor expose human sin, but bypass it. But the message of the cross proclaims to each one of us, even the best and most pious: You are a sinner, you are in a wrong relationship with God and hence with your neighbor also. You are seeking yourself. You wish to appear clever, and to attain the highest by means of your own intrinsic powers.

But why, you may ask, must we make so much ado about human sin? It is because in our inmost being we have each gone astray: I am godless, loveless, self-seeking, God-escaping. This is not manifested merely in those obvious weaknesses and vices that everyone condemns and with which, to a very large extent, we ourselves can deal. No, sin – the corruption of our nature – lies much deeper and is manifest even when we are occupied with the highest and holiest things.

The message of the cross goes to the root of our ills, and it alone can cure them radically. Just for that reason it spells folly and scandal. How? In the Bible it is not we who find a way to God; it is God who comes to us. It says nothing about practicing mystical introspection, of otherworldliness, of cultivating the interior life, with a view to reaching ultimately the divine ground of the soul. It is not a question of our own performances and exercises as a result of which we might hope to become pious and well-pleasing to God. That, in the last analysis, is self-praise. The central point of scripture is that God has mercy on us who are stuck so fast in the mire – if I may be pardoned the expression – that we cannot help ourselves.

We know why so many refuse to hear this message and why they can make neither head nor tail of it. The person for whom his reasoning power furnishes the supreme criterion of truth cannot believe that truth exists which does not flow from his own intellectual activity; truth which we cannot, by our own powers of recognition, apprehend, or by our powers of reason demonstrate; truth which does not dovetail into our own systems of thought and which lies entirely beyond the reach of our capacities. All this clashes greatly with our pride.

Still more serious than its folly is the offensiveness of the gospel's message. The Greeks sought after wisdom; the Jews desired by their good works to merit favor with God. Has not the thought come to you: Well, what then remains for us to do? What room is there for our own exertions, our own sense of responsibility?

Look once again at the revolt of our natural pride, this time not the pride of reason, but pride in our moral powers and in our determination to get things done for ourselves. Consider once more what it is that God bestows upon us. He imparts to us his love, communion with himself, and the fact that sin, which causes the deepest, most inward separation from him, is done away. How could the person who truly appropriates that gift become frivolous and irresponsible? Can one really receive the love of God without henceforth living in the strength of that love?

ALL MAN-MADE RELIGION stands in opposition to the gospel. It is an ascent toward the eternal, perfect God. Up, up–that is its call. God is high above, we are down below; and now we shall soar by means of our moral, spiritual, and religious endeavors out of the earthly, human depths into the divine heights.

God is too high and the evil in us too deep for us to reach the goal this way. Our souls become crippled and cramped by trying to rise to the highest height. The end is despair, or a self-righteousness that leaves room neither for love of God nor for love of others.

So if we are honest, we have to say that we cannot reach the goal. We cannot become what we ought to become, true men and women. Many let the matter rest there; they confess it, but take no action. They make themselves satisfied with half because they cannot have the whole. God demands all, not just half. And this "all" we are not capable of giving. What is impossible for us is what God wants—all love to him and to our fellow humans. If this is true, it would seem that we can have no good conscience, no trusting relationship with God, no inner peace, and no freedom of the soul.

But God has in his mercy shown us a different way. "You cannot come up to me, so I will come down to you." And God descends to us human beings. This act of becoming one of us begins at Christmas and ends on Good Friday.

God goes to the end. He reaches the goal. To be sure, this end is exactly the opposite of what we fix as our goal. We wish to climb up to heaven; God, however, descends—down to where? To death on the cross. This is why Jesus Christ had to descend into hell. He had to go the way to its very end. Our rightful end is hell, that is, banishment from God—godforsakenness. Only there has God completely come to us, there where he has taken upon himself everything, even the cursed end of our way.

Jesus Christ has gone into hell in order to get us out of there. For with everything he does, that is his goal, that he may get us out, reconcile us with God, and fill us with God's Spirit. He had to despair of God for us ("My God, my God, why have you forsaken me?") so that we do not have to despair of God. He has taken this upon himself so that we may become free of it.

16

Truth to Tell

Barbara Brown Taylor

We say we want to forget the world, but in the depths of our hearts we do not want to be forgotten by it.

FRANCOIS FENELON

THERE ARE MANY WAYS to tell the story of what happened on Good Friday. According to John, it involved a collusion between religion and politics. While Pilate and the chief priests conspired to solve their mutual problem while managing to remain enemies, Jesus stood at the center of the stage like a mirror in which all those around him saw themselves clearly for who they were. One way we Christians have avoided seeing our own reflections in the mirror is to pretend that this is a story about Romans and Jews. As long as they remain the villains, then we are off the hook – or so we think. Unfortunately, this is not a story that happened long ago in a land far away.

Sons and daughters of God are killed in every generation. They have been killed in holy wars and inquisitions, concentration camps and prison cells. They have been killed in Cape Town, Memphis, El Salvador and Alabama. The charges against them have run the gamut, but treason and blasphemy have headed the list, just as they did for Jesus. He upset those in charge at the courthouse and the temple. He suggested they were not doing their jobs. He offered himself as a mirror they could see themselves in, and they were so appalled by what they saw that they smashed it. They smashed him every way they could.

One of the many things this story tells us is that Jesus was not brought down by atheism and anarchy. He was brought down by law and order allied with religion, which is always a deadly mix. Beware those who claim to know the mind of God and who are prepared to use force, if necessary, to make others conform. Beware those who cannot tell God's will from their own. Temple police are always a bad sign. When chaplains start wearing guns and hanging out at the sheriff's office, watch out. Someone is about to have no king but Caesar.

This is a story that can happen anywhere at any time, and we are as likely to be the perpetrators as the victims. I doubt that many of us will end up playing Annas, Caiaphas or Pilate, however. They may have been the ones who gave Jesus the death sentence, but a large part of him had already died before they ever got to him—the part Judas killed off, then Peter, then all those who fled. Those are the roles with our names on them—not the enemies but the friends.

Whenever someone famous gets in trouble, that is one of the first things the press focuses on. What do his friends do? Do they support him or do they tell reporters that, unfortunately, they had seen trouble coming for some time? One of the worst things a friend can say is what Peter said. *We weren't friends, exactly. Acquaintances might be a better word. Actually, we just worked together. For the same company, I mean. Not together, just near each other. My desk was near his. I really don't know him at all.*

No one knows what Judas said. In John's Gospel he does not say a word, but where he stands says it all. After he has led some 200 Roman soldiers and the temple police to the secret garden where Jesus is praying, Judas stands with the militia. Even when Jesus comes forward to identify himself, Judas does not budge. He is on the side with the weapons and the handcuffs, and he intends to stay there.

Or maybe it was not his own safety that motivated him. Maybe he just fell out of love with Jesus. That happens sometimes. One day you think someone is wonderful and the next day he says or does something that makes you think twice. He reminds you of the difference between the two of you and you start hating him for that—for the difference—enough to begin thinking of some way to hurt him back.

I remember being at a retreat once where the leader asked us to think of someone who represented Christ in our lives. When it came time to share our answers, one woman stood up and said, "I had to think hard about that one. I kept thinking, Who is it who told me the truth about myself so clearly that I wanted to kill him for it?" According to John, Jesus died because he told the truth to everyone he met. He *was* the truth, a perfect mirror in which people saw themselves in God's own light.

What happened then goes on happening now. In the presence of his integrity, our own pretense is exposed. In the presence of his constancy, our cowardice is brought to light. In the presence of his fierce love for God and for us, our own hardness of heart is revealed. Take him out of the room and all those things become relative. I am not that much worse than you are nor you than I, but leave him in the room and there is no room to hide. He is the light of the world. In his presence, people either fall down to worship him or do everything they can to extinguish his light.

A cross and nails are not always necessary. There are a thousand ways to kill him, some of them as obvious as choosing where you will stand when the showdown between the weak and the strong comes along, others of them as subtle as keeping your mouth shut when someone asks you if you know him.

Today, while he dies, do not turn away. Make yourself look in the mirror. Today no one gets away without being shamed by his beauty. Today no one flees without being laid bare by his light.

17

They Took My Lord Away

John Donne

"THEY HAVE TAKEN AWAY my Lord, and I know not where they have laid him." This was one strain of Mary Magdalene's lamentation when she found not her Savior in the monument. It is a lamentable case to be fain to cry so, "They have taken"; other men have taken away Christ, by a dark and corrupt education. But when the casting away of God which is so often complained of by God in the prophets is pronounced against you, when you have had Christ offered to you by the motions of his grace and sealed to you by his sacraments, and yet will cast him so far from you that you know not where to find him; when you have poured him out at your eyes in profane and counterfeit tears which should be your soul's rebaptizing for your sins; when you have blown him away in corrupt and ill intended sighs, which should be the voice of the turtle-dove to sound your peace and reconciliation with your God; yes, when you have spit him out of your mouth in execrable and blasphemous oaths; when you have not only cast him so far as that you know not where to find him, but have made so ordinary and so indifferent a thing of sin as you know not when you did lose him, no, nor do not remember that ever you had him; no, nor do not know that there is any such man as Jesus, that is your Lord; the taking away is dangerous, when others hide Christ from you, but the casting away is desperate, when you yourself cast him away.

To lose Christ may befall the most righteous person that is; but then he knows where he left him; he knows at what time he lost his way, and where to seek it again. Even Christ's imagined father and his true mother, Joseph and Mary, lost him, and lost him in the holy city at Jerusalem. They lost him and knew it not. They lost him and went a day's journey without him and thought him to be in the company. But as soon as they comprehended their error, they sought and they found him, when as his mother told him, his father and she had sought with a heavy heart.

Alas we may lose him at Jerusalem, even in his own house, even at this moment while we pretend to do him service. We may lose him by suffering our thoughts to look back with pleasure upon the sins which we have committed, or to look forward with greediness upon some sin that is now in our purpose and prosecution. We may lose him at Jerusalem, how much more, if our dwelling be a Babylon in confusion and mingling God and the world together, or if it be a Sodom, a wanton and intemperate misuse of God's benefits to us. We may think him in the company when he is not; we may mistake his house; we may take a conventicle for a Church; we may mistake his apparel, that is, the outward form of his worship; we may mistake the person, that is, associate ourselves to such as are no members of his body.

But if we do not return to our diligence to seek him, and seek him, and seek him with a heavy heart, though we began with a taking away – other men, other temptations took him away – yet we end in a casting away, we ourselves cast him away since we have been told where to find him and have not sought him. And let no one be afraid to seek or find him for fear of the loss of good company; faith is no sullen thing, it is not a melancholy, there is not so sociable a thing as the love of Christ Jesus.

It was the first word which he who first found Christ of all the Apostles, St. Andrew, is noted to have said, "We have found the Messiah"; and it is the first act that he is noted to have done, after he had found him, to seek his brother Peter and take him to Jesus, so communicable a thing is the love of Jesus when we have found him.

But where are we likeliest to find him? It is said by Moses of the words and precepts of God, "They are not hid from thee, neither are they far off." Not in heaven that you should say, Who shall go up to heaven for us to bring them down? Nor beyond the seas, that you should go over the sea for them. But the word is very near you, even in your mouth and in your heart; and so near is Christ Jesus, or you shall never find him.

You must not so seek him in heaven, as that you cannot have immediate access to him without inter-cession of others, nor so beyond the sea as to seek him in a foreign Church, either where the Church is but an antiquary's cabinet full of rags and fragments of antiquity but nothing fit for that use for which it was first made, or where it is so new-built a house with bare walls that it is yet unfurnished of such ceremonies as should make it comely and revered. Christ is at home with you, he is at home within you, and there is the nearest way to find him.

18

Remember Her

Ernesto Cardenal

The place was Solentiname, an archipelago in Lake Nicaragua; the setting, a campesino worship meeting in the mid-1970s. The community gathered weekly under the leadership of Padré Cardenal, the priest.

IT WAS IN BETHANY. When they were sitting at the table a girl approached Jesus and poured perfume on his head.

> When the disciples saw this, they were angry and they began to say, "Why this waste? This could have been sold for much money to help the poor."

Oscar: If they'd sold it, it would have gone to only a small number of the poor, and the poor of the world are countless. On the other hand, when she offered it to Jesus, she was giving it, in his person, to all the poor. That made it clear it was Jesus we believe in. And believing in Jesus makes us concerned about other people, and we'll even get to create a society where there'll be no poor. Because if we're Christians there shouldn't be any poor.

William: But all that perfume. And the bottle. The alabaster bottle!

Padré: The alabaster bottle was sealed, and it had to be broken to use the perfume. The perfume could be used only once. And the Gospel says the whole house was filled with the fragrance of nard. It's believed that nard was an ointment that came from India.

Teresita: Maybe a smuggler paid her with that.

Maria: Jesus was a poor man, too, and he too deserved to have the perfume poured on him.

Padré: And worse off than poor, for they were going to kill him two days later. In the passage before this, Jesus said that it was two days to Passover. And in the following passage it's told that Judas went away from there to make the bargain to sell him.

A student from Managua: The Magdalene was used to that perfumed life, and things like that, and so she's being grateful according to her way of life. She's accustomed to a life of perfumes, jewels, carousing. And she pours perfume on him because that's the life she led, she thinks that's logical.

William: She's accustomed to squandering everything on the man she loves. And she doesn't have that economical mentality of the others. She squanders it right there. And she's not making economical calculations, like Judas.

Donald: The criticism must have been because that perfume was one of the most costly, but for her it was still cheap to spend it on Jesus, because of what Jesus had done for her earlier. She wasn't paying even a quarter of what she owed him.

José (Maria's husband, who works in the San José Bank): But Jesus hasn't forgotten the poor, because he says they will always have the poor among them. He means that if they want to help the poor they can be helping them a lot, later. They'll have the opportunity to give everything to the poor.

> Jesus heard this and said to them: "Why do you bother this woman? This thing that she has done is a good thing. The poor you will always have among you, but you will not always have me."

Bosco: That's stupid.

Laureano: That's a pretty weak answer because to say you're always going to have the poor is pretty silly.

Padré: But isn't it true that we've always had them?

Laureano: But we're not always *going* to have them.

William: This is a phrase much used by reactionaries to say there'll always have to be poor people, because Christ said so. The world can't really change, because according to Jesus there'll always have to be rich and poor.

Padré: He doesn't say there'll always be poor. Let's read it again.

Myriam (reads): "The poor you will always have among you."

William: And the "always"? How must we interpret that "always"?

Padré: Very simply. As long as there are poor, they will always be among us, we shall not be separated from them. Because the Christian community must be with the poor.

William: But there's that "always." Are there always going to be poor people? That's what disturbs me.

Padré: He says they are never going to be separated from the poor. That's not the same as saying there'll never stop being poor people. As long as there are poor, they'll always have them at their side, and among them.

Tomas Peña: When there's no more poor they won't.

A student: I've got it! He says "among you." He's referring to *them*, to his disciples, but that doesn't mean there'll never fail to be poor; he's not talking to all of humanity.

Laureano: Well, it was the disciples that he was saying that to. The disciples always have to be among the poor; they couldn't be among the rich.

Tomas Peña: There's lots of ways of being poor: a poor person can be somebody with an arm missing. A poor person is somebody born stupid, or an orphan child. These will be in the community. There'll always be people like that in need, but of course if we're Christian they won't be poor, in poverty; if they're among us, that is, we won't ever let them perish.

Olivia: It could also be that he was telling them instead, it seems to me, that there wouldn't be rich people, that everybody had to become poor.

Felipe: It seems that if things are well-distributed there can't be any rich; then everybody's poor.

Padré: I think what Jesus is saying is that he's going away but that in place of him the poor are left. What that woman was doing with him, they'd have to do later with the poor, because he wasn't going to be there any longer, or rather, we were going to have his presence in the poor. But can it be forever that he'll not be there?

The Gospel speaks of a second coming. He was going away and he was coming back.

Felipe: When there's that society that we dream about, that's when he's coming back, and we'll have him, and there won't be any poor people.

Padré: Helpless orphans, people who have to go begging, or that sleep under a tree, or die in the streets the way the consumptives die in Managua, that's what's not going to exist when he comes. People for whom you ought to sell a bottle of perfume if you have one.

Myriam: And pouring perfume on anybody will be the same as pouring it on Christ.

William: This passage has also been used to justify big spending for luxury in churches. Because Jesus accepted the pouring of perfume on him.

Olivia: But what that woman did was a lesson for us, and a reminder, so that what's spent in great temples that are good for nothing can be better spent on people, on the poor people he left behind.

Felipe: Those who now want to spend a lot on church buildings and not on the poor, they're repeating what Judas did in opposing pouring perfume on Jesus. Judas did it because he wanted to get the money, and the people that now want all the spending for the churches, it's for the same reason, because they live off that money. They're thieves.

> What this woman has done, in pouring this perfumed oil on my body, is to prepare me for my burial. I tell you, that wherever this good news is announced throughout the world, what this woman did will also be told, so that you may remember her.

Padré: Whenever his violent death is remembered, with no funeral, like the death of any subversive, they will remember what that woman did, as part of the good news.

Olivia: It seems to me that the remembering is for us also to do what she did. So that we do it now, not to him anymore, but to the poor. Or to him in the person of the poor. That's why we must remember her. That woman gave up a luxury. And people like us who don't have perfumes or luxurious things to give because we're poor?

Felipe: We can give other valuable things that we have.

Laureano: We can offer our lives as Jesus did. Then it will also be for us, that perfume that the woman poured on Jesus.

19

Merchandising Truth

Meister Eckhart

Jesus entered the temple area and drove out all who were buying and selling there.
MATTHEW 21:12

WE READ IN THE GOSPEL how Holy Week began with Jesus entering the temple and driving out all those that bought and sold. He then rebuked the vendors of doves: "Get these things out of here!" He was so crystal clear in his command that it was as if he said, "I have a right to this temple and I alone will be in it and have control of it."

What does this have to say to us? The temple God wants to be master of is the human soul, which he created and fashioned just like himself. We read that God said, "Let us make man in our own image." And he did it. He made each soul so much like himself that nothing else in heaven or on earth resembles him as much. That is why God wants the temple to be pure, so pure that nothing should dwell there except he himself. And that is the reason why he is so pleased when we really prepare our souls for him. When we do this, when he alone dwells in our hearts, he takes great comfort.

But who, exactly, are the people who buy and sell? Are they not precisely the good people? See! The merchants are those who only guard against mortal sins. They strive to be good people who do their good deeds to the glory of God, such as fasting, watching, praying and the like – all of which are good – and yet do these things so that God will give them something in exchange. Their efforts are contingent upon God doing something they ardently want to have done.

They are all merchants. They want to exchange one thing for another and to trade with our Lord. But they will be cheated out of their bargain – for what they have or have attained is actually given to them by God. Lest we forget, we do what we do only by the help of God, and so God is never obligated to us. God gives us nothing and does nothing except out of his own free will. What we are we are because of God, and whatever we have we receive from God and not by our own contriving. Therefore God is not in the least obligated to us—neither for our deeds nor for our gifts. He gives to us freely. Besides, Christ himself says, "Without me, you can do nothing."

People are very foolish when they want to trade with God. They know little or nothing of the truth. And God will strike them and drive them out of the temple. Light and darkness cannot exist side by side. God himself is the truth. When he enters the temple, he drives out ignorance and darkness and reveals himself in light and truth. Then, when the truth is known, merchants must depart—for truth wants no merchandising!

God does not seek his own benefit. In everything he acts only out of love. Thus, the person who is united with God lives the same way—he is innocent and free. He lives for love without asking why, and solely for the glory of God, never seeking his own advantage. God alone is at work in him.

As long as we look for some kind of pay for what we do, as long as we want to get something from God in some kind of exchange, we are like the merchants. If you want to be rid of the commercial spirit, then by all means do all you can in the way of good works, but do so solely for the praise of God. Live as if you did not exist. Expect and ask nothing in return. Then the merchant inside you will be driven out of the temple God has made. Then God alone dwells there. See! This is how the temple is cleared: when a person thinks only of God and honors him alone. Only such a person is free and genuine.

Jesus went into the temple and drove out those that bought and sold. His message was bold: "Take this all away!" But observe that when all was cleared, there was nobody left but Jesus. And when he is alone he is able to speak in the temple of the soul. Observe this also, for it is certain. If anyone else is speaking in the temple of the soul, Jesus keeps still, as if he were not at home. And he is not at home wherever there are strange guests – guests with whom the soul holds conversation, guests who always seek to bargain. If Jesus is to speak and be heard the soul must be alone and quiet.

And what does Jesus say when the soul has been cleared? His word is a revelation of himself and everything the Father has said to him. He reveals the Father's majesty with unmeasured power. If in your spirit you discover this power, you will possess a like power in whatever you do – a power that will enable you to live undividedly and pure. Neither joy nor sorrow, no, nor any created thing will be able to disrupt your soul. For Christ will remain and he will cast aside all that is insignificant and futile.

When Jesus is united with your soul, the soul's tide moves back again into its own, out of itself and above all things, with grace and power back to its prime origin. Then your fallen, fleshly self will become obedient to your inner, spiritual self, and you will in turn have a lasting peace in serving God without condition or demand.

20

Sheath Your Sword

John Dear

Then the men stepped forward, seized Jesus and arrested him. With that, one of Jesus' companions reached for his sword, drew it out and struck the servant of the high priest, cutting off his ear. "Put your sword back in its place," Jesus said to him, "for all who draw the sword will die by the sword."

MATTHEW 26:50–52

THE SOLDIERS AND THE AUTHORITIES lay hands on Jesus and arrest him. At that moment of confrontation, according to Luke, all the disciples ask, "Lord, shall we strike with a sword?" (Luke 22:49). Then Matthew's, Mark's, and Luke's unnamed disciple attempts to defend Jesus by using the same means as the arresting authorities. John's Gospel, however, goes further by naming the sword-wielding disciple as none other than Peter himself. Shortly thereafter, this Peter, who is willing to kill to protect Jesus, will deny three times that he even knows Jesus. Perhaps Peter, like the disciples and the rest of us, resorts to violence because he is more interested in protecting himself than in protecting Jesus.

The disciples are unable to comprehend Jesus' way of nonviolence. Over and over, Jesus instructs them to love their enemies and to lay down their lives for one another, thus preparing them for confrontation with the ruling authorities and the inevitable outcome. But the disciples never understand Jesus. They hear his Sermon on the Mount, and they celebrate the Passover meal with him. But they keep asking, "Lord, shall we strike with a sword?"

I have to go easy on the disciples, though, because I know how slow I am in my own heart to accept Jesus' way of the cross. Today, priests, bishops, theologians, cardinals, popes, monks, religious, and Christians of every stripe still ask, "Lord, shall we strike with a sword?" When wars heat up, revolutions foment, and violence threatens, we call out, "Lord, shall we strike with a sword?"—and rarely does anyone wait for an answer. To the patriotic mind, there can be only one answer: "Yes."

The swords and guns and bombs come out, and people are stabbed, shot, napalmed, electrocuted, gassed, obliterated, decimated. We strike with a sword – and so much more. We cut off an ear – and so much more. We destroy entire countries and incinerate hundreds of thousands of people in a flash. In fact, we are willing to risk the destruction of the entire planet, if necessary, to defend ourselves. Again and again, we strike back with violence to protect ourselves. We carry on, thanks to the ever-present, ever-trusty, ever-faithful, sword.

At this climactic point in the story of Jesus, as the soldiers put their hands on him, arrest him, and take him away, Jesus turns to the disciples for the final time. As he is dragged away by the authorities, he tells his community once again to reject violence:

> Put your sword back into its sheath, for all who take the sword will perish by the sword. Do you think that I cannot call upon my Father and he will not provide me at this moment with more than twelve legions of angels? But then how would the scriptures be fulfilled which say that it must come to pass in this way? (Matthew 26:52–55)

Jesus invokes God and God's nonviolent armies (the thousands of angels) who would answer if called, but he keeps his eye on the Scriptures. He will not become a murderous, imperial messiah; he is the nonviolent Suffering Servant of Isaiah. He is a peacemaking, sacrificial God.

Put your sword back! These are the last words—a definitive rebuke—the disciples hear from Jesus before they run away. If ever there was a moment in God's eyes when violence would be justifiable, this is it! But Jesus is clear: *Put your sword back!* His followers are not allowed to respond with violence. They are not allowed to kill. They are not allowed to harm others. They are not allowed to threaten others. They are not permitted to "deter" violent crime with the use of violence.

Why? Because all those who take up the sword shall perish by the sword. Violence begets violence. Killing begets killing. Nukes beget more nukes. Death begets death. Jesus, the incarnation of the God of nonviolence, stands for life. He will not succumb to the way of violence. Although he knows that he will perish under the cross's violence, he places his hope in the God of Life and awaits that third day.

Put your sword back! The command stands as the ultimate reproof of violence. From Christ's perspective—the perspective of one who is under arrest and in trouble with the authorities—our violence reveals that we have sided with the empire, that we are no different from the oppressive authorities. But Jesus, wanting us to break free from the cycle of violence, outlaws violent retaliation. Earlier, he surpasses Isaiah's vision of "beating swords into plowshares" by calling his followers to love their enemies. Now, when the authorities seize him, his command remains urgent but more modest: "Put back your sword." He will not permit violence under any circumstances. Luke's translation makes an equally all-encompassing, blanket condemnation of violence: *"Stop, no more of this!"* (Luke 22:51)

Those of us who would follow Jesus are precluded from drawing the sword. We are people who love our enemies; who prefer to undergo violence rather than inflict it upon others; who reject every form of violence, from nuclear weapons to chemical weapons to Trident submarines to handguns. We oppose the Stealth Bomber, the B52, the F22, the MX, the cruise missile, the latest nuclear technology, Livermore Laboratories, the S.A.C. Base, the marines, the CIA, the FBI, the army, the navy, and all perpetrators of violence and their arsenals. We renounce war and violent self-defense, tear up the just-war theory, and embrace gospel nonviolence. We not only put back any swords we have, but we beat them into plowshares. The unarmed Christ disarms us. Christ's community, the Church, is a community of nonviolence.

Does this mean that Christians cannot be employed by the Pentagon, the police, or the nuclear-weapons manufacturers? The question goes to the heart of Jesus' message. If we will obey the last words of Jesus, then we will not, like Judas, side with the imperial authorities—and we will not employ their means of violence. We will refuse to carry weapons, even for the noblest reason, and we will not work for any institution that inflicts violence. We prepare, instead, to undergo what Christ undergoes.

Jesus issues this final command—and his disciples turn and run away. They run not only from the imperial authorities who threaten the entire discipleship community; they run from the unarmed, nonviolent Christ who will not defend himself against personal harm. They know that an unarmed response to the imperial authorities will lead to disappearance, torture, and execution—and who can stomach such craziness? The Evangelists do not cover up the rejection Jesus undergoes: *All the disciples left him and fled.* Jesus is left alone once again, for the last time. He is led away to be slaughtered.

21

Believing Is Seeing

Romano Guardini

Thomas declared, "Unless I see the nail marks in his hands and put my finger where the nails were, and put my hand into his side, I will not believe it." **JOHN 20:25**

THOMAS APPEARS to have been a realist—reserved, cool, perhaps a little obstinate.

The days went by, and the disciples went on living under this considerable tension.

Another week, and they were together again in the house, and this time Thomas was with them. The same thing repeated itself. Jesus passed through closed doors, stepped into their midst, and spoke: "Peace be upon you!" Then he called the man who was struggling against faith: "Let me have thy finger; see, here are my hands. Let me have thy hand; put it into my side. Cease thy doubting, and believe!" At this point Thomas was overwhelmed. The truth of it all came home to him: this man standing before him, so moving, arousing such deep feelings within him, this man so full of mystery, so different from all other men—He is the very same One they used to be together with, who was put to death a short time ago. And Thomas surrendered: "Thou art my Lord and my God!" Thomas believed.

Then we come upon the strange words: "And Jesus said to him, 'Thou hast learned to believe, Thomas, because thou hast seen me. Blessed are those who have not seen, and yet have learned to believe!'"

Such words as these are really extraordinary! Thomas believed because he saw. But our Lord did not call him blessed. He had been allowed to "see," to see the hands and the side, and to touch the blessed wounds, yet he was not blessed!

Perhaps Thomas had a narrow escape from a great danger. He wanted proofs, wanted to see and touch; but then, too, it might have been rebellion deep within him, the vainglory of an intelligence that would not surrender, a sluggishness and coldness of heart. He got what he asked for: a look and a touch. But it must have been a concession he deplored having received, when he thought on it afterwards. He could have believed and been saved, not because he got what he demanded; he could have believed because God's mercy had touched his heart and given him the grace of interior vision, the gift of the opening of the heart, and of its surrender.

God could also have let him stay with the words he had spoken: in that state of unbelief which cuts itself off from everything, that insists on human evidence to become convinced. In that case he would have remained an unbeliever and gone on his way. In that state, external seeing and touching would not have helped him at all, he simply would have called it delusion. Nothing that comes from God, even the greatest miracle, can be proven like 2 x 2=4. It touches one; it is only seen and grasped when the heart is open and the spirit purged of self. Then it awakens faith. But when these conditions are not present there are always reasons to be found to say solemnly and impressively that it is all delusion, or that such-and-such is so because some other thing is so. Or, the excuse that always is handy: We cannot explain it yet...the future will enlighten us about it!

Thomas was standing a hairsbreadth away from obduracy and perdition. He was not at all blessed.

Blessed indeed are "those who have not seen, and yet have learned to believe!" Those who ask for no miracles, demand nothing out of the ordinary, but who find God's message in everyday life. Those who require no compelling proofs, but who know that everything coming from God must remain in a certain ultimate suspense, so that faith may never cease to require daring. Those who know that the heart is not overcome by faith, that there is no force or violence there, compelling belief by rigid certitudes. What comes from God touches gently, comes quietly; does not disturb freedom; leads to quiet, profound, peaceful resolve within the heart.

And those are called blessed who make the effort to remain open-hearted. Who seek to cleanse their hearts of all self-righteousness, obstinacy, presumption, inclination to "know better." Who are quick to hear, humble, free-spirited. Who are able to find God's message in the gospel for the day, or even from the sermons of preachers with no message in particular, or in phrases from the Law they have heard a thousand times, phrases with no quality of charismatic power about them, or in the happenings of everyday life which always end up the same way: work and rest, anxiety – and then again some kind of success, some joy, an encounter, and a sorrow.

Blessed are those who can see the Lord in all these things!

22

Turning

Henry Drummond

The Lord turned and looked straight at Peter…and Peter went outside and wept bitterly.   **LUKE 22:61–62**

EVERY PERSON AT SOME TIME in his life has fallen. Many have fallen many times; few, few times. And who of us can fail to shudder at the tale of Peter's guilt?

We are well aware of how the plot thickens round him. When we read the story for ourselves we feel an almost unconscious sympathy with Peter, as if his story has happened in our own lives. And we know, as we follow the dreary stages of his fall, these same well-worn steps have been traced ever since then by every human foot. Anyone who possesses an inner history can surely understand how Peter could have slept in the garden, when he should have watched and prayed. Who of us would dare to look down upon the faithlessness that made him follow Christ far off, instead of keeping at his Master's side? For we know too well what it means to get out of step with Christ. Wouldn't we, like the worldly company who warmed themselves by the fire and to our shame, be quick to question Peter?

Those of us who know the heart's deceit would surely find it difficult to judge this man—this man who had lived so long in the inner circle of fellowship with Christ, whose eyes were used to seeing miracles, who witnessed the glory of the transfiguration; this man whose ears were yet full of the most solemn words the world had ever heard, whose heart was warm still with Communion-table thoughts. We understand how he could have turned his back upon his Lord, and, almost ere the sacramental wine was dry upon his lips, curse him to his face. Such things, alas, are not strange to those of us who know the appalling tragedy of sin.

But there is something in Peter's life that is much greater than his sin. It is his repentance. We all too easily relate to Peter in his sin, but few of us grasp the wonder of his repentance. Sinful Peter is one man, and repentant Peter is another; and many of us who kept his company along these worn steps to sin have left him to trace the tear-washed path of repentance alone. But the real lesson in Peter's life is one of repentance. His fall is a lesson in sin that requires no teacher, but his repentance is a great lesson in salvation. And it is this great lesson that contains the only true spiritual meaning to those who have personally made Peter's discovery – that they have betrayed our God.

What then can we learn from Peter's turning around? First, it was not Peter who turned. It was the Lord who turned and looked at Peter. When the cock crew, that might have kept Peter from falling further. But he was just in the very act of sin. And when a person is in the thick of his sin his last thought is to throw down his arms and repent. So Peter never thought of turning, but the Lord turned. And when Peter would rather have looked anywhere else than at the Lord, the Lord looked at Peter. This scarce-noticed fact is the only sermon needed to anyone who sins – that the Lord turns first.

For this reason it is important to distinguish between two kinds of sorrow for sin. The one has to do with feeling sorry over some wrong or sin we have committed. This feeling seems to provide a sort of guarantee that we are not disposed to do the same wrong again, and that our better self is still alive enough to enter its protest against the sin our lower self has done. And we count this feeling of reproach, which treads so closely on the act, as a sort of compensation or atonement for the wrong.

In this kind of sorrow, however, there is no real repentance, no true sorrow for sin. It is merely wounded self-love. It is a sorrow over weakness, over the fact that when we were put to the test we found to our chagrin that we had failed. But this chagrin is what we are apt to mistake for repentance. This is nothing but wounded pride—sorrow that we did not do better, that we were not so good as we and others thought. It is just as if Peter turned and looked upon Peter. And when Peter turns and looks upon Peter, he sees what a poor, weak creature Peter is. And if God had not looked upon Peter he might have wept well-nigh as bitterly, not because he had sinned against his God, but because he, the great apostle, had done a weak thing—he was weak as other men.

All this amounts to little more than vexation and annoyance with ourselves, that, after all our good resolutions and attempts at reformation, we have broken down again. This kind of sorrow bears no lasting fruit, and is certainly far removed from the publican's prayer of repentance in the temple. "Lord be merciful to me, a sinner!" Stricken before his God, this publican had little thought of the self-respect he had lost. He certainly felt it no indignity to take the culprit's place.

All this is to say that there is a vast difference between divine and human sorrow. True contrition occurs when God turns and looks upon us. Human sorrow is us turning and looking upon ourselves. True, there is nothing wrong in turning and looking at oneself–only there is a danger. We can miss the most authentic experience of life in the imitation. For genuine repentance consists of feeling deeply our human helplessness, of knowing how God comes to us when we are completely broken.

In the end, it is God looking into the sinner's face that matters. Knowing first hand the difference between human and divine sorrow is of utmost importance. It is the distinction Luke brings out in the prodigal son's life, between coming to himself and coming to his father. "He came to himself," and then "he came to his father." So we are always coming to ourselves. We are always finding out, like the prodigal, the miserable bargains we have made. But this is not the crucial thing. Only when we come to our Father in response to his waiting look can we be freed and forgiven.

Peter turned around, but note well that it was the result of a mere glance. The Lord did not thunder and lightning at Peter to make him hear his voice. A look, and that was all. But it rent Peter's heart as lightning could not, and melted into his soul. God did not drive the chariot of his omnipotence up to Peter and command him to repent. God did not threaten. He did not even speak to him. That one look laid a spell upon his soul.

We misunderstand God altogether if we think he deals coarsely with our souls. If we consider what has really influenced our lives, we will find that it lies in a few silent voices that have preached to us, the winds which have passed across our soul so gently that we scarce could tell when they were come or gone. Even in the midst of the battle, when coarser weapons fail, let us not forget the lesson of Elijah: "A great and powerful wind tore the mountains apart and shattered the rocks before the Lord, but the Lord was not in the wind. After the wind there was an earthquake, but the Lord was not in the earthquake. After the earthquake came a fire, but the Lord was not in the fire. And after the fire came a gentle whisper" (1 Kings 19:11–12).

When God speaks he speaks so loudly that all the voices of the world seem dumb. And yet when God speaks he speaks so softly that no one hears the whisper but yourself. Today, perhaps, the Lord is turning and looking at you. Right where you are, your spirit is far away just now, dealing with some sin, some unbearable weight; and God is teaching you the lesson himself—the bitterest, yet the sweetest lesson of your life, in heart-felt repentance. Stay right where you are. Don't return into the hustle and bustle of life until the Lord has also turned and looked on you again, as he looked at the thief upon the cross, and until you have beheld the "glory of the love of God in the face of Jesus."

23

The Crucified

Kahlil Gibran

To make of his story something that could neither startle, nor shock, nor terrify, nor excite, nor inspire a living soul is to crucify the Son of God afresh.   **DOROTHY SAYERS**

TODAY, AND ON THIS SAME DAY of each year, man is startled from his deep slumber and stands before the phantoms of the Ages, looking with tearful eyes toward Mount Calvary to witness Jesus the Nazarene nailed on the Cross. But when the day is over and eventide comes, he returns and kneels to pray before the idols erected upon every hilltop, every prairie, and every barter of wheat.

Today, the Christian souls ride on the wing of memories and fly to Jerusalem. There they will stand in throngs, beating upon their bosoms, and staring at him, crowned with a wreath of thorns, stretching his arms before heaven, and looking from behind the veil of Death into the depths of Life.

But when the curtain of night drops over the stage of the day and the brief drama is concluded, the Christians will go back in groups and lie down in the shadow of oblivion between quilts of ignorance and slothfulness.

On this one day of each year, the philosophers leave their dark caves, and the thinkers their cold cells, and the poets their imaginary arbors, and all stand reverently upon that silent mountain, listening to the voice of a young man saying of his killers, "Oh Father, forgive them, for they know not what they are doing."

But as dark silence chokes the voices of the light, the philosophers and the thinkers and the poets return to their narrow crevices and shroud their souls with meaningless pages of parchment.

The women who busy themselves in the splendor of Life will bestir themselves today from their cushions to see the sorrowful woman standing before the Cross like a tender sapling before the raging tempest; and when they approach near to her, they will hear a deep moaning and a painful grief.

The young men and women who are racing with the torrent of modern civilization will halt today for a moment, and look backward to see the young Magdalene washing with her tears the blood stains from the feet of a Holy Man suspended between heaven and earth; and when their shallow eyes weary of the scene they will depart and soon laugh.

On this day of each year, Humanity wakes with the awakening of Spring, and stands crying below the suffering Nazarene; then she closes her eyes and surrenders herself to a deep slumber. But Spring will remain awake, smiling and progressing until merged into Summer, dressed in scented golden raiment. Humanity is a mourner who enjoys lamenting the memories and heroes of the Ages. If Humanity were possessed of understanding, there would be rejoicing over their glory. Humanity is like a child standing in glee by a wounded beast. Humanity laughs before the strengthening torrent which carries into oblivion the dry branches of the trees, and sweeps away with determination all things not fastened to strength.

Humanity looks upon Jesus the Nazarene as a poor-born who suffered misery and humiliation with all the weak. And he is pitied, for Humanity believes he was crucified painfully. And all that Humanity offers to him is crying and wailing and lamentation. For centuries Humanity has been worshiping weakness in the person of the Savior.

The Nazarene was not weak! He was strong and is strong! But people refuse to heed the true meaning of strength.

Jesus never lived a life of fear, nor did he die complaining. He lived as a leader; he was crucified as a crusader; he died with a strength that frightened his killers and tormentors.

Jesus was not a bird with broken wings. He was a raging tempest who broke all crooked wings. He feared not his persecutors nor his enemies. Free and brave and daring he was. He defied all despots and oppressors. He saw the contagious pustules and amputated them. He muted Evil and he crushed Falsehood and he choked Treachery.

Jesus came not from the heart of the circle of Light to destroy the homes and build upon their ruins the convents and monasteries. He did not persuade the strong man to become a monk or a priest, but he came to send forth upon this earth a new spirit, with power to crumble the foundation of any monarchy built upon human bones and skulls. He came to demolish the majestic palaces, constructed on the graves of the weak, and crush the idols, erected upon the bodies of the poor. Jesus was not sent here to teach the people to build magnificent churches and temples amidst the cold wretched huts and dismal hovels. He came to make the human heart a temple, and the soul an altar, and the mind a priest.

These were the missions of Jesus the Nazarene, and these are the teachings for which he was crucified. And if Humanity were wise, she would stand today and sing in strength the song of conquest and the hymn of triumph.

Oh, Crucified Jesus, who art looking sorrowfully from Mount Calvary at the sad procession of the Ages, and hearing the clamor of the dark nations, and understanding the dreams of Eternity: Thou art, on the Cross, more glorious and dignified than one thousand kings upon one thousand thrones in one thousand empires.

Thou art, in the agony of death, more powerful than one thousand generals in one thousand wars.

With thy sorrows, thou art more joyous than Spring with its flowers.

With thy suffering, thou art more bravely silent than the crying of angels of heaven. Before thy lashers, thou art more resolute than the mountain of rock.

Thy wreath of thorns is more brilliant and sublime than the crown of Bahram. The nails piercing thy hands are more beautiful than the scepter of Jupiter.

The spatters of blood upon thy feet are more resplendent than the necklace of Ishtar.

Forgive the weak who lament thee today, for they do not know how to lament themselves.

Forgive them, for they do not know that thou hast conquered death with death, and bestowed life upon the dead.

Forgive them, for they do not know that thy strength still awaits them.

Forgive them, for they do not know that every day is thy day.

Passion

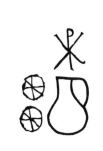

BENEATH THY CROSS

Christina Rossetti

Am I a stone, and not a sheep,
    That I can stand, O Christ, beneath Thy cross,
To number drop by drop Thy Blood's slow loss,
    And yet not weep?

Not so those women loved
    Who with exceeding grief lamented Thee;
Not so fallen Peter weeping bitterly;
    Not so the thief was moved;

Not so the Sun and Moon
    Which hid their faces in a starless sky,
A horror of great darkness at broad noon –
    I, only I.

Yet give not o'er,
    But seek Thy sheep, true Shepherd of the flock;
Greater than Moses, turn and look once more
    And smite a rock.

24

The Mystery of Jesus

Blaise Pascal

JESUS SUFFERS IN HIS PASSION the torments inflicted upon him by men, but in his agony he suffers the torments which he inflicts on himself. *He was troubled*. This punishment is inflicted by no human, but an almighty hand, and only he that is almighty can bear it.

Jesus seeks some comfort at least from his three dearest friends, and they sleep: he asks them to bear with him a while, and they abandon him with complete indifference, and with so little pity that it did not keep them awake even for a single moment. And so Jesus was abandoned to face the wrath of God alone.

Jesus is alone on earth, not merely with no one to feel and share his agony, but with no one even to know of it. Heaven and he are the only ones to know.

Jesus is in a garden, not of delight, like the first Adam, who there fell and took with him all mankind, but of agony, where he has saved himself and all mankind.

He suffers this anguish and abandonment in the horror of the night.

I believe that this is the only occasion on which Jesus ever complained. But then he complained as though he could no longer contain his overflowing grief: "My soul is exceeding sorrowful, even unto death."

Jesus seeks companionship and solace from men.

It seems to me that this is unique in his whole life, but he finds none, for his disciples are asleep.

Jesus will be in agony until the end of the world. There must be no sleeping during that time.

Jesus, totally abandoned, even by the friends he had chosen to watch with him, is vexed when he finds them asleep because of the dangers to which they are exposing not him but themselves, and he warns them for their own safety and their own good, with warm affection in the face of their ingratitude. And warns them: "The spirit is willing but the flesh is weak."

Jesus, finding them asleep again, undeterred by consideration either for him or for themselves, is kind enough not to wake them up and instead lets them take their rest.

Jesus prays, uncertain of the will of the Father, and is afraid of death. But once he knows what it is, he goes to meet it and offer himself up. "'Let us be going.' He went forth" (John 18:4).

Jesus asked of men and was not heard.

Jesus brought about the salvation of his disciples while they slept. He has done this for each of the righteous while they slept, in nothingness before their birth and in their sins after their birth.

He prays only once that the cup might pass from him, even then submitting himself to God's will, and twice that it should come if it must be so.

Jesus, weary at heart.

Jesus, seeing all his friends asleep and all his enemies watchful, commends himself utterly to his Father.

Jesus disregards the enmity of Judas, and sees only in him God's will, which he loves; so much so that he calls him friend.

Jesus tears himself away from his disciples to enter upon his agony: we must tear ourselves away from those who are nearest and dearest to us in order to imitate him.

While Jesus remains in agony and cruelest distress, let us pray longer.

We implore God's mercy, not so that he shall leave us in peace with our vices, but so that he may deliver us from them…

"Take comfort; you would not seek me if you had not found me."

"I thought of you in my agony: I shed these drops of blood for you."

"It is tempting me rather than testing yourself to wonder if you would do right in the absence of this or that protection. I will accomplish righteousness in you if hardship comes."

"Let yourself be guided by my rules. See how well I guided the Virgin and the saints who let me work in them."

"The Father loves all I do."

"Do you want it always to cost me the blood of my humanity while you do not even shed a tear?"

"My concern is for your conversion; do not be afraid, and pray with confidence as though for me."

"I am present with you through my word in Scripture, my spirit in the church, through inspiration…and my prayer among the faithful."

"Physicians will not heal you, for you will die in the end, but it is I who will heal you and make your body immortal."

"Endure the chains and bondage of the body. For the present I am delivering you from spiritual bondage."

"I am a better friend to you than this man or that, for I have done more for you than they, and they would never endure what I have endured from you, and they would never die for you, while you were being faithless and cruel, as I did, and as I am ready to do, and still do in my elect, and in the Blessed Sacrament."

"If you knew your sins, you would lose heart." – "In that case I shall lose heart, Lord, for I believe in their wickedness on the strength of your assurance." – "No, for I who tell you this can heal you, and the fact that I tell you is a sign that I want to heal you. As you expiate them you will come to know them, and you will be told: 'Behold, thy sins are forgiven thee.'"

"Repent then of your secret sins and the hidden evil of those you know."

"Lord, I give you all."

"I love you more ardently than you have loved your foulness."

"May mine be the glory, not thine, worm and clay…"

Pilate's false justice only causes Jesus Christ to suffer. For he has him scourged in the name of "justice," then put to death. It would have been better to put him to death at once. The falsely righteous are like that. They do both good works and bad in order to please the world and in so doing they are not wholly Christ's, for they are ashamed to be. Finally, when it comes to great temptations and opportunities, they put him to death.

I see the depths of my pride, curiosity, concupiscence. There is no link between me and God or Jesus Christ the righteous. But he was made sin for me. All your scourges fell upon him. He is more abominable than I, and, far from loathing me, feels honored that I go to him and help him. But he healed himself and will heal me all the more surely. I must add my wounds to his, and join myself to him, and he will save me in saving himself. But no wounds must be added for the future...

25

Prisoner of Hope

Jürgen Moltmann

In the sickness of his agony, the will of Jesus arises perfect at last; and of itself, unsupported now, declares—a naked consciousness of misery hung in the waste darkness of the universe—declares for God, in defiance of pain, of death, of apathy, of self, of negation, of the blackness within and around it; calls aloud upon the vanished God. **GEORGE MACDONALD**

THE NIGHT BEFORE THE ROMANS arrested him, Jesus went into the garden of Gethsemane, taking only three of his friends with him, and "began to be greatly distressed and troubled," as Mark writes. "He began to be sorrowful and afraid," Matthew reports. In fact, "He despaired." "My soul is very sorrowful, even to death," he said, and begged his friends to stay awake with him.

Earlier, too, Christ had often withdrawn at night in order to be united in prayer with the God whom he always called so intimately "my Father." Here, for the first time, he does not want to be alone with God. He seeks protection among his friends. Protection from whom? And then comes the prayer that sounds like a demand: "Father, all things are possible to thee; remove this cup from me" (Mark 14:36) – spare me this suffering. What suffering? In Matthew and Luke the prayer sounds somewhat more modest: "If it be possible…" and "If thou art willing," remove this cup from me.

Christ's request *was not granted*. God, his Father, rejected it. Elsewhere we are always told "I and the Father are *one*." But here Christ's communion with God seems to break down. Christ's true passion begins with the prayer in Gethsemane which was not heard, which was rejected through the divine silence; for his true passion was his suffering from God.

Of course there was also the simple human fear of pain. But I believe that it was quite a different fear which laid hold of Christ here and lacerated his soul. It was the fear that he, the only begotten Son, who loved the Father as no one had ever loved before, could be "forsaken," "rejected," even "cursed" by that Father. He is not afraid for his life. He is afraid for God. He is afraid for the Father's kingdom, whose joy he had proclaimed to the poor.

This *suffering from God himself* is the real torment in Christ's passion. This godforsakenness is the cup which he is not spared. God's terrible silence in response to Christ's prayer in Gethsemane is more than a deathly stillness. It is echoed in the dark night of the soul, in which everything that makes life something living withers away, and in which hope vanishes. Martin Buber called it the eclipse of God.

Who can stay awake in this night of God? Who will not be as if paralyzed by it? Jesus' friends were protected from its terrors by a profound sleep. Luke, the doctor, and other witnesses speak of a "bloody sweat" which fell on the ground from the wakeful, imploring Christ. The Luther Bible heads this chapter "The Struggle in Gethsemane." The struggle with whom? Christ's struggle with himself? His struggle with death? I think it is more than that. It is Christ's struggle with God. This was his real agony. He overcame it through his self-surrender. That was his victory, and our hope.

AT THE END OF CHRIST'S PASSION, on Golgotha, the place of execution, we hear a despairing cry to God. "And at the ninth hour Jesus cried with a loud voice, 'Eloi, Eloi, lama sabachthani,' which means, 'My God, my God, why has thou forsaken me?'"

For three hours he hung nailed to the cross, apparently in silence, locked in agony and waiting for death. And then he died with this cry, which expresses the most profound abandonment by the God on whom he had pinned all his hopes and for whom he was hanging on the cross.

We shall never be able to get used to the fact that at the very center of the Christian faith we hear this cry of the godforsaken Christ for God. We shall always attempt to weaken its effect and to replace it by "more pious" parting words. What Christ was afraid of, what he wrestled with in Gethsemane, what he implored the Father to save him from, was not spared him. It happened on the cross. The Father forsook the Son and "God is silent." The Son was forsaken by the Father, rejected and cursed. He bore the judgment in which everyone is alone and in which no one can stand.

Is there any answer to the question *why* God forsook him? Is there any answer to the agonizing questionings of disappointment and death: "My God, Why? Why…?"

A real answer to this question cannot be a theoretical answer beginning with the word "Because." It has to be a practical answer. An experience of this kind can only be answered by another experience, not by an explanation. A reality like this can be answered only by another reality. It is the answer of resurrection: "For a brief moment I forsook you, but with great compassion I will gather you."

At the center of the Christian faith is the history of Christ's passion. At the center of this passion is the experience of God endured by the godforsaken, God-cursed Christ. Is this the end of all human and religious hope? Or is it the beginning of the true hope, which has been born again and can no longer be shaken?

For me it is the beginning of true hope, because it is the beginning of a life which has death behind it and for which hell is no longer to be feared.

At the point where men and women lose hope, where they become powerless and can do nothing more, the lonely, assailed and forsaken Christ waits for them and gives them a share in his passion.

The passionately loving Christ, the persecuted Christ, the lonely Christ, the Christ despairing over God's silence, the Christ who in dying was so totally forsaken, for us and for our sakes, is like the brother or the friend to whom one can confide *everything*, because he knows everything and has suffered everything that can happen to us—and more.

In our hopes about life, in our activity, in our love of living, we participate in his passion for the kingdom of freedom.

Our disappointments, our lonelinesses and our defeats do not separate us from him; they draw us more deeply into communion with him. And with the final unanswered cry, "Why, my God, why?" we join in his death cry and await with him the resurrection.

This is what faith really is: believing, not with the head or the lips or out of habit, but believing *with one's whole life*. It means seeking community with the human Christ in every situation in life, and in every situation experiencing his own history. Good Friday is the most comprehensive and most profound expression of Christ's fellowship with every human being.

In him the despair that oppresses us becomes free to hope. The arrogance with which we hinder ourselves and other people melts away, and we become as open and as vulnerable as he was.

What initially seemed so meaningless and so irreconcilable – our hope and Christ's cross – belong together as a single whole, just as do the passionate hope for life and the readiness for disappointment, pain and death.

Beneath the cross of Christ hope is born again out of the depths. The person who has once sensed this is never afraid of any depths again. His hope has become firm and unconquerable: "Lord, I am a prisoner – a prisoner of hope!"

26

A Father's Grief

Martin Luther

LET US SAY AGAIN: Into God as God, no pain, grief, or dislike can come. Yet God is grieved on account of our sin.

Since grief cannot be in God outside the creature, it occurs when God is in man or in a divine man.

Sin is such a pain to God, it saddens him so much, that he would himself be tortured and bodily die so that he might thereby wipe out a person's sin.

If we asked God if he would live so that sin should remain, or die in order to destroy sin, he would choose death.

For God feels more pain over our sin and it gives him more grief than his own torture and death.

Now, if one person's sin causes God pain, how much more, then, the sins of all people? So you see how deeply we grieve God with our sins.

Where God is man, he does not grieve over anything but sin. Nothing else gives real pain.

For all that is or occurs without sin, that is what God will have and be.

Yet grief of sorrow over sin should and must remain in a divine person until he leaves his body in death, even if he were to live until the latter day, or forever.

From this came Christ's hidden anguish of which no one reports or knows but Christ himself. Therefore we call it what it is: hidden.

This hidden sorrow over our sinful condition is an attribute of God's that he has chosen and that he is pleased to see in man. But it is God's attribute above all. Sorrow over sin does not finally belong to us humans; we ourselves are not capable of it. Wherever God can bring it about in us, it is the most pleasing and most appropriate but at the same time the most bitter and heavy undertaking on which we can enter.

What we have been describing here is one of God's attributes, which he would like to see realized in us. For it is we who should practice it and put it into effect. The true Light teaches us about sorrow over sin; it teaches us moreover, that we, in whom it is put into effect and practiced, should claim that divine mood for ourselves as little as though we were not there.

For then we recognize with inner knowledge that we ourselves would not be capable of creating the awareness of sin and that it does not belong to us.

27

Shared Hells

Peter Kreeft

I could never myself believe in God, if it were not for the cross. The only God I believe in is the one Nietzsche ridiculed as "God on the Cross." In the real world of pain, how could one worship a God who was immune to it? I have entered many Buddhist temples and stood respectfully before the statue of Buddha, his legs crossed, arms folded, eyes closed, the ghost of a smile playing round his mouth, a remote look on his face, detached from the agonies of the world. But each time after a while I have had to turn away. And in imagination I have turned instead to that lonely, twisted, tortured figure on the cross, nails through hands and feet, back lacerated, limbs wrenched, brow bleeding from thorn-pricks, mouth dry and intolerably thirsty, plunged in God-forsaken darkness. That is the God for me! He laid aside his immunity to pain. He entered our world of flesh and blood, tears and death. He suffered for us. **JOHN STOTT**

CALVARY IS JUDO. The enemy's own power is used to defeat him. Satan's craftily orchestrated plot, rolled along according to plan by his agents Judas, Pilate, Herod, and Caiaphas, culminated in the death of God. And this very event, Satan's conclusion, was God's premise. Satan's end was God's means. God won Satan's captives—us—back to himself by freely dying in our place.

It is, of course, the most familiar, the most often-told story in the world. Yet it is also the strangest, and it has never lost its strangeness, its awe, and will not even in eternity, where angels tremble to gaze at things we yawn at. And however strange, it is the only key that fits the lock of our tortured lives and needs. We needed a surgeon, he came and reached into our wounds with bloody hands. He didn't give us a placebo or a pill or good advice. He gave us himself.

He came. He entered space and time and suffering. He came, like a lover. He did the most important thing and he gave the most important gift: himself. It is a lover's gift. Out of our tears, our waiting, our darkness, our agonized aloneness, out of our weeping and wondering, out of our cry, "My God, my God, why hast

Thou forsaken me?" he came, all the way, right into that cry.

He sits beside us in the lowest places of our lives, like water. Are we broken? He is broken with us. Are we rejected? Do people despise us not for our evil but for our good, or attempted good? He was "despised and rejected of men." Do we weep? Is grief our familiar spirit, our horrifyingly familiar ghost? Do we ever say, "Oh, no, not again! I can't take it any more!"? Do people misunderstand us, turn away from us? They hid their faces from him as from an outcast, a leper. Is our love betrayed? Are our tenderest relationships broken? He too loved and was betrayed by the ones he loved. "He came unto his own and his own received him not."

Does it seem sometimes as if life has passed us by or cast us out, as if we are sinking into uselessness and oblivion? He sinks with us. He too is passed over by the world. His way of suffering love is rejected, his own followers often the most guilty of all; they have made his name a scandal, especially among his own chosen people. What Jew finds the road to him free from the broken weapons of bloody prejudice? We have made it nearly impossible for his own people to love him, to see him as he is, free from the smoke of battle and holocaust.

How does he look upon us now? With continual sorrow, but never with scorn. We add to his wounds. There are two thousand nails in his cross. We, his beloved and longed for and passionately desired, are constantly cold and correct and distant to him. And still he keeps brooding over the world like a hen over an egg, like a mother who has had all of her beloved children turn against her. "Could a mother desert her young? Even so I could not desert you." He sits beside us not only in our sufferings but even in our sins. He does not turn his face from us, however much we turn our face from him.

Does he descend into all our hells? Yes. In the unforgettable line of Corrie ten Boom from the depths of a Nazi death camp, "No matter how deep our darkness, he is deeper still." Does he descend into violence? Yes, by suffering it and leaving us the solution that to this day only a few brave souls have dared to try, the most notable in our memory not even a Christian but a Hindu. Does he descend into insanity? Yes, into that darkness too. Even into the insanity of suicide? Can he be there too? Yes, he can. "Even the darkness is not dark to him." He finds or makes light even there, in the darkness of the mind – though perhaps not until the next world, until death's release.

Love is why he came. It's all love. The buzzing flies around the cross, the stroke of the Roman hammer as the nails tear into his screamingly soft flesh, the infinitely harder stroke of his own people's hammering hatred, hammering at his heart – why? For love. God is love, as the sun is fire and light, and he can no more stop loving than the sun can stop shining.

Henceforth, when we feel the hammers of life beating on our heads or on our hearts, we can know – we must know – that he is here with us, taking our blows. Every tear we shed becomes his tear. He may not yet wipe them away, but he makes them his. Would we rather have our own dry eyes, or his tear-filled ones? He came. He is here. That is the salient fact. If he does not heal all our broken bones and loves and lives now, he comes into them and is broken, like bread, and we are nourished. And he shows us that we can henceforth use our very brokenness as nourishment for those we love. Since we are his body, we too are the bread that is broken for others. Our very failures help heal other lives; our very tears help wipe away tears; our being hated helps those we love. When those we love hang up on us, he keeps the lines open.

God's answer to the problem of suffering not only really happened two thousand years ago, but it is still happening in our own lives. The solution to our suffering is our suffering! All our suffering can become part of his work, the greatest work ever done, the work of salvation, of helping to win for those we love eternal joy.

28

For the Sacrificed

Dag Hammarskjöld

A YOUNG MAN, adamant in his committed life. The one who was nearest to him relates how, on the last evening, he arose from supper, laid aside his garments, and washed the feet of his friends and disciples – an adamant young man, alone as he confronted his final destiny.

He had observed their mean little play for his – his! – friendship. He knew that not one of them had the slightest conception why he had to act in the way that he must. He knew how frightened and shaken they would all be. And one of them had informed on him, and would probably soon give a signal to the police.

He had assented to a possibility in his being, of which he had had his first inkling when he returned from the desert. If God required anything of him, he would not fail. Only recently, he thought, had he begun to see more clearly, and to realize that the road of possibility might lead to the Cross. He knew, though, that he had to follow it, still uncertain as to whether he was indeed "the one who shall bring it to pass," but certain that the answer could only be learned by following the road to the end. The end *might* be a death without significance – as well as being the end of the road of possibility.

Well, then, the last evening. An adamant young man: "Know ye what I have done to you?...And now I have told you before it comes to pass...One of you shall betray me...Whither I go, ye cannot come...Will'st thou lay down thy life for my sake? Verily I say unto thee: the cock shall not crow...My peace I give unto you...That the world may know that I love the Father, and as the Father gave me commandment, even so I do...Arise, let us go hence."

Is the hero of this immortal, brutally simple drama in truth "the Lamb of God that taketh away the sins of the world"? Absolutely faithful to a divined possibility – in that sense the Son of God, in that sense the sacrificial Lamb, in that sense the Redeemer. A young man, adamant in his commitment, who walks the road of possibility to the end without self-pity or demand for sympathy, fulfilling the destiny he has chosen – even sacrificing affection and fellowship when the others are unready to follow him – into a new fellowship.

FOR THE SACRIFICED – in the hour of sacrifice – only one thing counts: faith – alone among enemies and skeptics. Faith, in spite of the humiliation which is both the necessary precondition and the consequence of faith, faith without any hope of compensation other than he can find in a faith which reality seems so thoroughly to refute.

Would the Crucifixion have had any sublimity or meaning if Jesus had seen himself crowned with the halo of martyrdom? What we have later added was not there for him. And we must forget all about it if we are to hear his commands.

29

God the Rebel

G. K. Chesterton

Our faith begins at the point where atheists suppose it must be at an end. Our faith begins with the bleakness and power which is the night of the cross, abandonment, temptation and doubt about everything that exists! Our faith must be born where it is abandoned by all tangible reality; it must be born of nothingness, it must taste this nothingness and be given it to taste in a way that no philosophy of nihilism can imagine. **H. J. IWAND**

THAT A GOOD MAN may have his back to the wall is no more than we knew already; but that God could have his back to the wall is a boast for all insurgents for ever. Christianity is the only religion on earth that has felt that omnipotence made God incomplete. Christianity alone has felt that God, to be wholly God, must have been a rebel as well as a king. Alone of all creeds, Christianity has added courage to the virtues of the Creator. For the only courage worth calling courage must necessarily mean that the soul passes a breaking point – and does not break.

In this indeed I approach a matter more dark and awful than it is easy to discuss; and I apologize in advance if any of my phrases fall wrong or seem irreverent touching a matter which the greatest saints and thinkers have justly feared to approach. But in that terrific tale of the Passion there is a distinct emotional suggestion that the author of all things (in some unthinkable way) went not only through agony, but through doubt. It is written, "Thou shalt not tempt the Lord thy God." No; but the Lord thy God may tempt himself; and it seems as if this was what happened in Gethsemane.

In a garden Satan tempted man: and in a garden God tempted God. He passed in some superhuman manner through our human horror of pessimism. When the world shook and the sun was wiped out of heaven, it was not at the crucifixion, but at the cry from the cross: the cry which confessed that God was forsaken of God.

And now let the revolutionists of this age choose a creed from all the creeds and a god from all the gods of the world, carefully weighing all the gods of inevitable recurrence and of unalterable power. They will not find another god who has himself been in revolt. Nay (the matter grows too difficult for human speech), but let the atheists themselves choose a god. They will find only one divinity who ever uttered their isolation; only one religion in which God seemed for an instant to be an atheist.

30

Thy Will Be Done

Edith Stein

"**THY WILL BE DONE**," in its full extent, must be the guideline for the Christian life. It must regulate the day from morning to evening, the course of the year, and the entire of life. Only then will it be the sole concern of the Christian. All other concerns the Lord takes over. This one alone, however, remains ours as long as we live. And, sooner or later, we begin to realize this. In the childhood of the spiritual life, when we have just begun to allow ourselves to be directed by God, we feel his guiding hand quite firmly and surely. But it doesn't always stay that way. Whoever belongs to Christ must go the whole way with him. He must mature to adulthood: he must one day or other walk the way of the cross to Gethsemane and Golgotha.

Will you remain faithful to the Crucified? Consider carefully! The world is in flames, the battle between Christ and the Antichrist has broken into the open. If you decide for Christ, it could cost you your life. Carefully consider what you promise.

Before you hangs the Savior on the cross, because he became *obedient* to death on the cross. He came into the world not to do his own will, but his Father's will. If you intend to be the bride of the Crucified, you too must completely renounce your own will and no longer have any desire except to fulfill God's will.

The Savior hangs naked and destitute before you on the cross because he has chosen *poverty*. Those who want to follow him must renounce all earthly goods. It is not enough that you once left everything out there and came to the monastery. You must be serious about it now as well. Gratefully receive what God's providence sends you. Joyfully do without what he may let you do without. Do not be concerned with your own body, with its trivial necessities and inclinations, but leave concern to those who are entrusted with it. Do not be concerned about the coming day and the coming meal.

The Savior hangs before you with a pierced heart. He has spilled his heart's blood to win your heart. If you want to follow him in holy *purity*, your heart must be free of every earthly desire. Jesus, the Crucified, is to be the only object of your longings, your wishes, your thoughts.

The world is in flames. Are you impelled to put them out? Look at the cross. From the open heart gushes the blood of the Savior. This extinguishes the flames of hell. Make your heart free by the faithful fulfillment of your vows; then the flood of divine love will be poured into your heart until it overflows and becomes fruitful to all the ends of the earth.

Do you hear the groans of the wounded on the battle-fields in the west and the east? You are not a physician and not a nurse and cannot bind up the wounds. You cannot get to them. Do you hear the anguish of the dying? You would like to be a priest and comfort them. Does the lament of the widows and orphans distress you? You would like to be an angel of mercy and help them. Look at the Crucified. If you are bound to him by the faithful observance of your holy vows, your being is precious blood. Bound to him, you are omnipresent as he is. You cannot help here or there like the physician, the nurse, the priest. You can be at all fronts, wherever there is grief, in the power of the cross. Your compassionate love takes you everywhere, this love from the divine heart. Its precious blood is poured everywhere, soothing, healing, saving.

The eyes of the Crucified look down on you, asking, probing. Will you make your covenant with the Crucified anew in all seriousness? What will you answer him?

"Lord, where shall we go? You have the words of eternal life."

31

Still Bleeding

Wendell Berry

Truth nailed upon the cross compels nobody, oppresses no one; it must be accepted and confessed freely; its appeal is addressed to free spirits. **NICHOLAS BERDYAEV**

The speaker is Jayber Crow in Berry's novel of the same name:

FOR A WHILE AGAIN I couldn't pray. I didn't dare to. In the most secret place of my soul I wanted to beg the Lord to reveal himself in power. I wanted to tell him that it was time for his coming. If there was anything at all to what he had promised, why didn't he come in glory with angels and lay his hands on the hurt children and awaken the dead soldiers and restore the burned villages and the blasted and poisoned land? Why didn't he cow our arrogance?…

But thinking such things was as dangerous as praying them. I knew who had thought such thoughts before: "Let Christ the king of Israel descend now from the cross, that we may see and believe." Where in my own arrogance was I going to hide?

Where did I get my knack for being a fool? If I could advise God, why didn't I just advise him (like our great preachers and politicians) to be on our side and give us victory? I had to turn around and wade out of the mire myself.

Christ did not descend from the cross except into the grave. And why not otherwise? Wouldn't it have put fine comical expressions on the faces of the scribes and the chief priests and the soldiers if at that moment he had come down in power and glory? Why didn't he do it? Why hasn't he done it at any one of a thousand good times between then and now?

I knew the answer. I knew it a long time before I could admit it, for all the suffering of the world is in it. He didn't, he hasn't, because from the moment he did, he would be the absolute tyrant of the world and we would be his slaves. Even those who hated him and hated one another and hated their own souls would have to believe in him then. From that moment the possibility that we might be bound to him and he to us and us to one another by love forever would be ended.

And so, I thought, he must forebear to reveal his power and glory by presenting himself as himself, and must be present only in the ordinary miracle of the existence of his creatures. Those who wish to see him must see him in the poor, the hungry, the hurt, the wordless creatures, the groaning and travailing beautiful world.

I would sometimes be horrified in every moment I was alone. I could see no escape. We are too tightly tangled together to be able to separate ourselves from one another either by good or by evil. We all are involved in all and any good, and in all and any evil. For any sin, we all suffer. That is why our suffering is endless. It is why God grieves and Christ's wounds still are bleeding.

32

On This Gallows

Dorothee Soelle

*Not what Christ has done for us but what we Christians, all
these centuries since he was here, have been doing to him.*

HARRY EMERSON FOSDICK

HOW CAN HOPE BE EXPRESSED in the face of senseless suffering? I begin with a story that Elie Wiesel, a
survivor of Auschwitz, relates in his book *Night:*

> The SS hung two Jewish men and a boy before the assem-
> bled inhabitants of the camp. The men died quickly but
> the death struggle of the boy lasted half an hour. "Where
> is God? Where is he?" a man behind me asked. As the
> boy, after a long time, was still in agony on the rope,
> I heard the man cry again, "Where is God now?" and

> I heard a voice within me answer, "Here he is—he is hanging here on this gallows…"

It is difficult to speak about this experience. But the decisive phrase, that God is hanging "here on this gallows," has two meanings. First, it is an assertion about God. God is no executioner—and no almighty spectator (which would amount to the same thing). God is not the mighty tyrant. Between the sufferer and the one who causes the suffering, between the victim and the executioner, God, whatever people make of this word, is on the side of the sufferer. God is on the side of the victim, he is hanged.

Second, it is an assertion about the boy. If it is not also an assertion about the boy, then the story is false and one can forget about the first assertion. But how can the assertion about the boy be made without cynicism? "He is with God, he has been raised, he is in heaven." Such traditional phrases are almost always clerical cynicism with a high apathy content. What language can preserve what is affirmed in classical theology and yet also be translated into a message of liberation? We would have to learn to hear the confession of the Roman centurion, "Truly this was God's son," in the phrase, "Here he is—he is hanging here on this gallows." Every single one of the six million was God's beloved son. Were anything else the case, resurrection would not have occurred, even in Jesus' case.

God is not in heaven; he is hanging on the cross. Love is not an otherworldly, intruding, self-asserting power—and to meditate on the cross can mean to take leave of that dream.

God has no other hands than ours. Even "the future," which today is often supposed to translate the mythical word "heaven," cannot alter the fact that the boy had to die that way in Auschwitz. It is no less significant for us than it is for the boy that God is the one hanging on this gallows. God had no other hands than ours, which are able to act on behalf of other children.

In this sense those who suffer in vain and without respect depend on those who suffer in accord with justice. If there were no one who said, "I die, but I shall live," no one who said, "I and the Father are one," then there would be no hope for those who suffer mute and devoid of hoping. All suffering would then be senseless, destructive pain that could not be worked on, all grief would be "worldly grief" and would lead to death. But we know of people who have lived differently, suffered differently. There is a history of resurrections, which has vicarious significance. A person's resurrection is no personal privilege for himself alone – even if he is called Jesus of Nazareth. It contains within itself hope for all, for everything.

33

From Action to Passion

Henri Nouwen

I WAS INVITED to visit a friend who was very sick. He was a man about fifty-three years old who had lived a very active, useful, faithful, creative life. Actually, he was a social activist who had cared deeply for people. When he was fifty he found out he had cancer, and the cancer became more and more severe.

When I came to him, he said to me, "Henri, here I am lying in this bed, and I don't even know how to think about being sick. My whole way of thinking about myself is in terms of action, in terms of doing things for people. My life is valuable because I've been able to do many things for many people. And suddenly, here I am, passive, and I can't do anything anymore." And he said to me, "Help me to think about this situation in a new way. Help me to think about my not being able to do anything anymore so I won't be driven to despair. Help me to understand what it means that now all sorts of people are doing things to me over which I have no control."

As we talked I realized that he and many others were constantly thinking, "How much can I still do?" Somehow this man had learned to think about himself as a man who was worth only what he was doing. And so when he got sick, his hope seemed to rest on the idea that he might get better and return to what he had been doing. If the spirit of this man was dependent on how much he would still be able to do, what did I have to say to him?…

The central word in the story of Jesus' arrest is one I never thought much about. It is "to be handed over." That is what happened in Gethsemane. Jesus was handed over. Some translations say that Jesus was "betrayed," but the Greek says he was "handed over." Judas handed Jesus over (see Mark 14:10). But the remarkable thing is that the same word is used not only for Judas but also for God. God did not spare Jesus, but handed him over to benefit us all (see Romans 8:32).

So this word, "to be handed over," plays a central role in the life of Jesus. Indeed, this drama of being handed over divides the life of Jesus radically in two. The first part of Jesus' life is filled with activity. Jesus takes all sorts of initiatives. He speaks; he preaches; he heals; he travels. But immediately after Jesus is handed over, he becomes the one to whom things are being done. He's being arrested; he's being led to the high priest; he's being taken before Pilate; he's being crowned with thorns; he's being nailed on a cross. Things are being done to him over which he has no control. That is the meaning of passion—being the recipient of other people's initiatives.

It is important for us to realize that when Jesus says, "It is accomplished," he does not simply mean, "I have done all the things I wanted to do." He also means, "I have allowed things to be done to me that needed to be done to me in order for me to fulfill my vocation." Jesus does not fulfill his vocation in action only but also in passion. He doesn't just fulfill his vocation by doing the things the Father sent him to do, but also by letting things be done to him that the Father allows to be done to him, by receiving other people's initiatives.

Passion is a kind of waiting—waiting for what other people are going to do. Jesus went to Jerusalem to announce the good news to the people of that city. And Jesus knew that he was going to put a choice before them: Will you be my disciple, or will you be my executioner? There is no middle ground here. Jesus went to Jerusalem to put people in a situation where they had to say "Yes" or "No." That is the great drama of Jesus' passion: he had to wait upon how people were going to respond. How would they come? To betray him or to follow him? In a way, his agony is not simply the agony of approaching death. It is also the agony of having to wait.

All action ends in passion because the response to our action is out of our hands. That is the mystery of work, the mystery of love, the mystery of friendship, the mystery of community—they always involve waiting. And that is the mystery of Jesus' love. God reveals himself in Jesus as the one who waits for our response. Precisely in that waiting the intensity of God's love is revealed to us. If God forced us to love, we would not really be lovers.

All these insights into Jesus' passion were very important in the discussions with my friend. He realized that after much hard work he had to wait. He came to see that his vocation as a human being would be fulfilled not just in his actions but also in his passion. And together we began to understand that precisely in this waiting the glory of God and our new life both become visible.

Precisely when Jesus is being handed over into his passion, he manifests his glory. "Whom do you seek?... I am he" are words that echo all the way back to Moses and the burning bush: "I am the one. I am who I am" (see Exodus 3:1–6). In Gethsemane, the glory of God manifested itself again, and they fell flat on the ground. Then Jesus was handed over. But already in the handing over we see the glory of God who hands himself over to us. God's glory revealed in Jesus embraces passion as well as resurrection.

"The Son of Man," Jesus says, "must be lifted up as Moses lifted up the serpent in the desert, so that everyone who believes may have eternal life in him" (John 3:14–15). He is lifted up as a passive victim, so the cross is a sign of desolation. And he is lifted up in glory, so the cross becomes at the same time a sign of hope. Suddenly we realize that the glory of God, the divinity of God, bursts through in Jesus' passion precisely when he is most victimized. So new life becomes visible not only in the resurrection on the third day, but already in the passion, in the being handed over. Why? Because it is in the passion that the fullness of God's love shines through. It is supremely a waiting love, a love that does not seek control.

When we allow ourselves to feel fully how we are being acted upon, we can come in touch with a new life that we were not even aware was there. This was the question my sick friend and I talked about constantly. Could he taste the new life in the midst of his passion? Could he see that in his being acted upon by the hospital staff he was already being prepared for a deeper love? It was a love that had been underneath all the action, but he had not tasted it fully. So together we began to see that in the midst of our suffering and passion, in the midst of our waiting, we can already experience the resurrection.

Imagine how important that message is for people in our world. If it is true that God in Jesus Christ is waiting for our response to divine love, then we can discover a whole new perspective on how to wait in life. We can learn to be obedient people who do not always try to go back to the action but who recognize the fulfillment of our deepest humanity in passion, in waiting. If we can do this, I am convinced that we will come in touch with the glory of God and our own new life. Then our service to others will include our helping them see the glory breaking through, not only where they are active but also where they are being acted upon.

34

I Thirst for You

Joseph Langford

I am the vessel.
The draught is God's.
And God is the thirsty one.
DAG HAMMARSKJÖLD

I KNOW YOU through and through—I know everything about you. The very hairs of your head I have numbered. Nothing in your life is unimportant to me, I have followed you through the years, and I have always loved you—even in your wanderings.

I know every one of your problems. I know your need and your worries. And yes, I know all your sins. But I tell you again that I love you—not for what you have or haven't done—I love you for you, for the beauty and dignity my Father gave you by creating you in his own image.

It is a dignity you have often forgotten, a beauty you have tarnished by sin. But I love you as you are, and I have shed my blood to win you back. If you only ask me with faith, my grace will touch all that needs changing in your life; and I will give you the strength to free yourself from sin and all its destructive power.

I know what is in your heart—I know your loneliness and all your hurts—the rejections, the judgments, the humiliations. I carried it all before you. And I carried it all for you, so you might share my strength and victory. I know especially your need for love—how you are thirsting to be loved and cherished. But how often have you thirsted in vain, by seeking that love selfishly, striving to fill the emptiness inside you with passing pleasures—with even greater emptiness of sin. Do you thirst for love? "Come to me all you who thirst" (John 7:37). I will satisfy you and fill you. Do you thirst to be cherished? I cherish you more than you can imagine to the point of dying on a cross for you.

I thirst for you. Yes, that is the only way to even begin to describe my love for you: *I thirst for you*. I thirst to love and to be loved by you—that is how precious you are to me. *I thirst for you.* Come to me, and fill your heart and heal your wounds.

If you feel unimportant in the eyes of the world, that matters not at all. For me, there is no one any more important in the entire world than you. *I thirst for you.* Open to me, come to me, thirst for me, give me your life—and I will prove to you how important you are to my heart.

No matter how far you may wander, no matter how often you forget me, no matter how many crosses you may bear in this life, there is one thing I want you to remember always, one thing that will never change: *I thirst for you*—just as you are. You don't need to change to believe in my love, for it will be your belief in my love that will change you. You forget me, and yet I am seeking you every moment of the day—standing at the door of your heart, and knocking.

Do you find this hard to believe? Then look at the cross, look at my heart that was pierced for you. Have you not understood my cross? Then listen again to the words I spoke there—for they tell you clearly why I endured all this for you: *I thirst* (John 19:28). Yes, I thirst for you—as the rest of the Psalm verse which I was praying says of me: "I looked for love, and I found none" (Psalm 69:20).

All your life I have been looking for your love—I have never stopped seeking to love and be loved by you. You have tried many other things in your search for happiness; why not try opening your heart to me, right now, more than you ever have before.

Whenever you do open the door of your heart, whenever you come close enough, you will hear me say to you again and again, not in mere human words but in spirit: "No matter what you have done, I love you for your own sake."

Come to me with your misery and your sins, with your trouble and needs, and with all your longing to be loved. I stand at the door of your heart and knock. Open to me, for *I thirst for you.*

Crucifixion

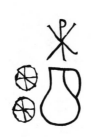

THIS BREAD I BREAK

Dylan Thomas

This bread I break was once the oat
This wine upon a foreign tree
Plunged in its fruit;
Man in the day or wind at night
Laid the crops low, broke the grape's joy.

Once in this wine the summer blood
Knocked in the flesh that decked the vine,
Once in this bread
The oat was merry in the wind;
Man broke the sun, pulled the wind down.

This flesh you break, this blood you let
Make desolation in the vein,
Were oat and grape
Born of the sensual root and sap;
My wine you drink, my bread you snap.

35

Our Mediator

Saint Augustine

The Maker of man was made man, that the Ruler of the stars might suck at the breast; that the Bread might be hungered; the Fountain, thirst; the Light, sleep; the Way, be wearied by the journey; the Truth, be accused by false witnesses; the Judge of the living and the dead, be judged by a mortal judge; the Chastener, be chastised with whips; the Vine, be crowned with thorns; the Foundation, be hung upon the tree; Strength, be made weak; Health, be wounded; life, die. To suffer these and suchlike things, undeserved things, that He might free the undeserving, for neither did He deserve any evil, who for our sakes endured so many evils, nor were we deserving of anything good, we who through Him received such good. **THE CONFESSIONS**

WHOM COULD I FIND to reconcile me to you? Should I go courting the angels? With what prayer or by what rites could I win them to my cause? The angels used magical powers to beguile their clients, who were seeking a mediator to purge them of their impurities, but found none; for there was no one there but the devil, disguised as an angel of light. Being without a fleshly body himself, he strongly appealed to the pride of fleshly humans. They were mortal and sinful, whereas you, Lord, to whom they sought, though proudly, to be reconciled, are immortal and without sin.

What we needed was a mediator to stand between God and men who should be in one respect like God, in another kin to human beings, for if he were manlike in both regards he would be far from God, but if Godlike in both, far from us: and then he would be no mediator. By the same token that spurious mediator, by whose means pride was deservedly duped in keeping with your secret decree, does have one thing in common with human beings, namely sin; and he appears to have something else in common with God because, not being clad in mortal flesh, he is able to flaunt himself as immortal. But in fact since death is the wage sin earns he has this in common with humans, that he lies under sentence of death as surely as they do.

In your unfathomable mercy you first gave the humble certain pointers to the true Mediator, and then sent him, that by his example they might learn even a humility like his. This Mediator between God and humankind, the man Christ Jesus, appeared to stand between mortal sinners and the God who is immortal and just: like us he was mortal, but like God he was just. Now the wage due to justice is life and peace; and so through the justice whereby he was one with God he broke the power of death on behalf of malefactors rendered just, using that very death to which he willed to be liable along with them. He was pointed out to holy people under the old dispensation that they might be saved through faith in his future passion, as we are through faith in that passion now accomplished. Only in virtue of his humanity is he the Mediator; in his nature as the Word he does not stand between us and God, for he is God's equal, God with God, and with him only one God.

How you loved us, O good Father, who spared not even your only Son, but gave him up for us evildoers! How you loved us, for whose sake he who deemed it no robbery to be your equal was made subservient, even to the point of dying on the cross! Alone of all he was free among the dead, for he had power to lay down his life and power to retrieve it. For our sake he stood to you as both victor and victim, and victor because victim; for us he stood to you as priest and sacrifice, and priest because sacrifice, making us sons and daughters to you instead of servants by being born of you to serve us. With good reason is there solid hope for me in him, because you will heal all my infirmities through him who sits at your right hand and intercedes for us. Were it not so, I would despair. Many and grave are those infirmities, many and grave; but wider-reaching is your healing power. We might have despaired, thinking your Word remote from any conjunction with human-kind, had he not become flesh and made his dwelling among us.

Filled with terror by my sins and my load of misery I had been turning over in my mind a plan to flee into solitude, but you forbade me, and strengthened me by your words. *To this end Christ died for all*, you reminded me, *that they who are alive may live not for themselves, but for him who died for them*. See, then, Lord: I cast my care upon you that I may live, and I will contemplate the wonders you have revealed. You know how stupid and weak I am: teach me and heal me. Your only

Son, in whom are hidden all treasures of wisdom and knowledge, has redeemed me with his blood. Let not the proud disparage me, for I am mindful of my ransom. I eat it, I drink it, I dispense it to others, and as a poor man I long to be filled with it among those who are fed and feasted. And then do those who seek him praise the Lord.

36

The Crucifix

Thomas Howard

To look at the Crucifix and then to look at our own hearts; to test by the cross the quality of our love—if we do that honestly and unflinchingly we don't need any other self-examination. The lash, the crown of thorns, the mockery, the stripping, the nails— life has equivalents of all these for us and God asks a love for himself and his children which can accept and survive all that in the particular way in which it is offered to us. It is no use to talk in a large vague way about the love of God; here is its point of insertion in the world. **EVELYN UNDERHILL**

THERE IS A POINT OF VIEW, widespread among non-Catholic Christians, that dismisses the Crucifix with the remark, "Oh—we worship a Risen Christ." This notion is not in itself wholly false, namely, that Good

Friday was not the end of the story. Easter followed forthwith. Indeed, indeed—the Christ we invoke in our prayers and supplications is not dead.

However, what the eye of faith perceives in the Crucifix is a mystery of such fathomless depth that the sun itself darkened and the rocks split apart. This is not an event to be set to one side in the interest of doctrinal punctilio. The fact that the Resurrection followed this dark event and brought it to fruition and filled it, paradoxically, with light and glory does not suggest to us that our devotion and our prayer ought not to unite themselves to this One in the very hour of his suffering when he most intimately bound himself to ours. It is a mistake to insist, with sprightly accuracy, that the One who thus suffered here is now risen, just as it is a mistake, with similar accuracy, to insist to the parents at the open grave of their child that we will all one day be raised. There is a time for everything under the sun.

We don't just have an empty cross with the work finished and done. Oh, to be sure, logic and chronology (and some rigorous theologies) will dictate that it is so. *Consummatum est.* Yes. We know that. We cling to that. But that which is thus "finished" remains present and actual in time—in the dimension, that is, under which we mortals must experience what it is to belong to the race of Adam. The victory of Easter, with its empty tomb and mighty risen Prince, cancels sin, suffering, and death: but we experience that canceling, not as a mathematical point that has no longevity, so to speak, but rather as the condition for our salvation, that is, the condition by which we are brought to glory. Brought: this bringing takes time. We live in time. We suffer in time. We see not yet all things put under Thee.

Sin, sorrow, and suffering, and death itself, were indeed taken away at the Cross, but we mortals must enter into the depths of this mystery in actual experience. The fact that the Savior bore all this for us does not mean that we bear nothing of it; rather, it means that we are invited in to that place (the Cross) where suffering is transfigured. We (the Church) are his Body, says St. Paul. As such, we share in his suffering for the life of the world.

Jesus tells his followers that they will drink the cup of which he drank and be baptized with the baptism with which he was to be baptized (he was speaking specifically of his imminent suffering in Jerusalem). Where, suddenly, is the theology that teaches that because the Savior did it all, we thereby are reduced to the status of inert bystanders? Whether the sorrow of the moment is a lost glove or a lost spouse or a bombed city, I am invited by the Divine Mercy to unite this terrible loss (for the child, the loss of the glove may threaten the end of the world) with the suffering of the Savior at Calvary and thus to discover that my suffering is his suffering, and that – paradox of paradoxes – his is ours (again – we are his Body).

The pain is there. It has not suddenly evaporated. The Cross is the Cross, not a magician's wand. And on that Cross we see the One whose self-offering transfigured all suffering. Stalingrad is still rubble: the Cross did not avert the Panzer howitzers. But insofar as I will bring my burden of sorrow and suffering (*and* sin: sins are indeed washed away here; this *corpus* is the *Agnus Dei* who taketh away the sin of the world) – insofar as I will bring my burden here, fall on my knees, and cry out for help, to that extent I may know that the Savior is receiving what I offer up and making it one with his own offering here.

This is what the saints speak of when they speak of suffering. The Divine Mercy, like alchemy, transforms the leaden burden into precious substance. We cannot know just what the experience of the martyrs was as the red-hot iron entered their flesh, but we know that they were enabled to bear the pain and even, incredibly, to sing and rejoice. It is all opaque—nonsense, even—to the squint of logic, but we hear the testimony of a thousand saints who have suffered, either physically or in the inner man, and who tell us, not merely of consolations, but of joy.

There is no guarantee of joy, of course: the darkness that shrouds Calvary is thick, and it is scarcely believable that the Son of God himself had it all sunshine in his Passion. We go through that valley of the shadow of death with him.

But *with him*. With whom? Him—the Savior—the *Agnus Dei*—this figure on the Cross.

This figure assists us to gather our wayward thoughts and feelings. It focuses things. It may even come to our rescue if words fail: the corpus, bowed in agony but with arms stretched wide, says, not in sentences but in its very shape, "Come unto me, all ye that labor and are heavy laden, and I will give you rest. Take my yoke upon you."

My burden of the moment may be sorrow: Warsaw, or a son debauched by his own choice. It may be physical suffering: paralysis, painful hospital tests, or arthritis.

Or it may be sin—my own, alas, or the evil that regales me wherever I look.

For this Crucifix bids me also to the place where my exasperation or ire over others' sins must be forsworn in the name of the Mercy that God himself offers to the perpetrators of sin (I being the chief among them). What is it that rouses my ire in the passing scene? Someone cutting into the line at the ticket window? Bloody-mindedness on the part of some driver on the freeway? Cretinous inefficiency on the part of committees, boards, and panels of experts in local, state, or federal government? Monumental waste of taxpayers' money on all sides? Cruelty to children, animals, or the poor? Poisonous ingratitude and self-absorption on the part of some old person being cared for? The list goes on and on.

And my ire seethes. Swift vengeance is what we want here, I say. Oh, for the power to set things right forthwith and finally. If I were in control...

The words die on my tongue as the Crucifix looms. Ah, *Domine Deus*. Depart from me, Lord: I am only a sinful man. Lord, I am not worthy. "With what judgment ye judge, ye shall be judged" (Matt. 7:2).

The judgment of my sins revealed itself at Calvary. Do I wish a separate, and stricter, judgment to come upon everyone else? Can I maintain such a wish as the figure on the Cross looks at me?

No. For in that look I am bidden to the region where all is forgiveness and for which I have been invited to prepare myself every time I have said "and forgive us our trespasses, as we forgive those who trespass against us." Not only have I not been asked to participate in judging the sins of others: I have been offered the noble opportunity to join my voice with that of the Crucified as he cries out, "Father, forgive them."

37

The Cross and the Cellar

Morton T. Kelsey

EACH OF US HAS underneath our ordinary personality, which we show to the public, a cellar in which we hide the refuse and rubbish which we would rather not see ourselves or let others see. And below that is a deeper hold in which there are dragons and demons, a truly hellish place, full of violence and hatred and viciousness. Sometimes these lower levels break out, and it is to this lowest level of humans that public executions appeal.

In the cross this level of our being has thrust itself up out of its deepest underground cellar so that we humans may see what is in all of us and take heed. The cross is crucial because it shows what possibilities for evil lie hidden in human beings. It is the concretion of human evil in one time and place. Whenever we look upon the cross, which was simply a more fiendish kind of gibbet, we see what *humankind* can do, has done, and still does to some human beings. It can make us face the worst in ourselves and in others, that part of us which can sanction a cross or go to watch a crucifixion. The cross is the symbol, alive and vivid, of the evil that is in us, of evil itself.

Scratch the surface of a person and below you find a beast or worse than a beast. (For animals seldom play with their victims.) This is what the cross says. We don't like to believe this, but let's look at the facts. Who were the ones who ran the concentration camps of Nazi Germany, kept the gas ovens fed, made lamp shades out of tatooed human skin, who performed the mass murders and executions? It is important to remember that Germany was the most literate and educated nation in the world. We think that the people who did these things must have been perverted monsters. Actually most of them, until they stepped into these roles, had been peaceful German burghers who had never hurt a person, living quietly and peacefully in their comfortable homes, and then the devils in them were let loose.

Were all the Mongol hordes which followed Genghis Khan just wild brutes? No, at home they were kind and loving to their wives and families, and yet as they swept through Persia they killed a hundred thousand in a single city. Once Attila died, the Huns became as gentle and peaceful as any people in Europe. And yet Genghis Khan, Tamerlane, Attila were novices, much less efficient and adroit at disposing of human life, compared with our educated moderns.

We don't want to face our own darkness; it is too painful. The atrocity stories which follow in the wake of every war, every one, involve both sides and are as incredible as the cross, and are usually performed by men and women who never before had done such things. Scratch the surface of a human being and the demons of hate and revenge, avarice and bestiality and sheer destructiveness break forth. The cross stands before us to remind us of this depth of ourselves so that we can never forget. These forces continue to break forth in many parts of the world now, and many of us would like to forget how in some places in the United States we treat a person whose skin is black. We like to forget Mai Lai and the napalm bombs and the tiger cages in Vietnam.

Again and again we read the stories of violence in our daily papers, of the mass murders and ethnic wars still occurring in numerous parts of our world. But how often do we say to ourselves: "What seizes people like that, even young people, to make them forget family and friends, and suddenly kill other human beings?" We don't always ask the question in that manner. Sometimes we are likely to think, almost smugly: "How different those horrible creatures are from the rest of us. How fortunate I am that I could never kill or hurt other people like they did."

I do not like to stop and, in the silence, look within, but when I do I hear a pounding on the floor of my soul. When I open the trap door into the deep darkness I see the monsters emerge for me to deal with. There emerges the sheer mindless destructive brutality of the Frankenstein monster, and next the deft and skilled Aztec priest sacrificing his victim. Then I see the image of the slave trader with his whips and chains and then Torquemada fresh from having burned his witch and then the accuser crying at me with a condemning voice. How painful it is to bear all this, but it is there to bear in all of us. Freud called it the death wish, Jung the demonic darkness. If I do not deal with it, it deals with me. The cross reminds me of all this.

This inhumanity of human to human is tamed most of the time by law and order in most of our communities, but there are not laws strong enough to make men and women simply cease their cruelty and bitterness. The cross symbolizes what ordinary people do when they fail to see the monsters dwelling deep within their lives. The person who talks viciously or plays the power game is stepping into the path of those who invented and practiced crucifixion. It is not a pretty way…

LET US LOOK at some of the people who brought Jesus of Nazareth to crucifixion. They were not monsters, but ordinary men and women like you and me.

Pilate receives most of the blame for Jesus' death, and yet Pilate didn't want to crucify the man. Why did Pilate condemn Jesus? Because Pilate was a coward. He cared more about his comfortable position than he did about justice. He didn't have the courage to stand for what he knew was right. It was because of this relatively small flaw in Pilate's character that Jesus died on a cross. Whenever you and I are willing to sacrifice someone else for our own benefit, whenever we don't have the courage to stand up for what we see is right, we step into the same course that Pilate took.

And Caiaphas, was he such a monster? Far from it. He was the admired and revered religious leader of the most religious people in that ancient world. He was the High Priest. His personal habits were impeccable. He was a devout and sincerely religious man. Why did he seek to have Jesus condemned? He did it for the simple reason that he was too rigid. He thought he had to protect God from this man, thought he had to protect the Jewish faith, and so he said: "It is good for one man to die instead of a nation being destroyed." Caiaphas's essential flaw was that he thought he had the whole truth. People who have fought religious wars, those who have persecuted in the name of religion, have followed in his footsteps. Those who put their creeds above mercy and kindness and love, walk there even now.

Why did Judas betray his master? He wasn't interested in the thirty pieces of silver, at least not primarily. Judas had wanted Jesus to call upon heavenly powers, to take control of the situation and throw the Romans out of Palestine. When he failed to do this, Judas no longer wanted anything to do with him. Judas' fault was that he couldn't wait. When we can't wait and want to push things through, when we think we can accomplish a noble end by human means, we are just like Judas.

Then there was the nameless carpenter who made the cross. He was a skilled workman. He knew full well what the purpose of that cross was. If you questioned him he probably would have said: "But I am a poor man who must make a living. If other men use it for ill, is it my fault?" So say all of us who pursue jobs which add nothing to human welfare or which hurt some people. Does the work I do aid or hinder human beings? Are we crossmakers for our modern world? There are many, many of them.

These were the things that crucified Jesus on Friday in Passover week A.D. 29. They were not wild viciousness or sadistic brutality or naked hate, but the civilized vices of cowardice, bigotry, impatience, timidity, falsehood, indifference—vices all of us share, the very vices which crucify human beings today.

This destructiveness within us can seldom be transformed until we squarely face it in ourselves. This confrontation often leads us into the pit. The empty cross is planted there to remind us that suffering is real but not the end, that victory still is possible if we strive on.

38

The Distance

Simone Weil

Oh, marvelous omnipotence of love! But God who creates out of nothing, who almightily takes from nothing and says, "Be," lovingly adjoins, "Be something even in opposition to me." Marvelous love, even his omnipotence is under the sway of love!
SØREN KIERKEGAARD

IT IS SOMETIMES EASY to deliver an unhappy person from his present distress, but it is difficult to set him free from his past affliction. Only God can do it. And even the grace of God itself cannot cure our irremediably wounded nature here below. The glorified body of Christ bore the marks of nails and spear.

One can only accept the existence of affliction by considering it at a distance.

God created through love and for love. God did not create anything except love itself, and the means to love. He created love in all its forms. He created beings capable of love from all possible distances. Because no other could do it, he himself went to the greatest possible distance, the infinite distance. This infinite distance between God and God, this supreme tearing apart, this agony beyond all others, this marvel of love, is the crucifixion. Nothing can be further from God than that which has been made accursed.

This tearing apart, over which supreme love places the bond of supreme union, echoes perpetually across the universe in the midst of the silence, like two notes, separate yet melting into one, like pure and heart-rending harmony. This is the Word of God. The whole creation is nothing but its vibration. When human music in its greatest purity pierces our soul, this is what we hear through it. When we have learned to hear the silence, this is what we grasp more distinctly through it.

Those who persevere in love hear this note from the very lowest depths into which affliction has thrust them. From that moment they can no longer have any doubt.

WE HAVE TO CROSS the infinite thickness of time and space – and God has to do it first, because he comes to us first. Of the links between God and man, love is the greatest. It is as great as the distance to be crossed.

So that the love may be as great as possible, the distance is as great as possible. That is why evil can extend to the extreme limit beyond which the very possibility of good disappears. Evil is permitted to touch this limit. It sometimes seems as though it overpassed it.

IN ORDER that we should realize the distance between ourselves and God, it was necessary that God should be a crucified slave. For we do not realize distance except in the downward direction. It is much easier to imagine ourselves in the place of God the Creator than in the place of Christ crucified.

THE DIMENSIONS of Christ's charity are the same as the distance between God and the creature.

The function of mediation in itself implies a tearing asunder. That is why we cannot conceive of the descent of God toward men or the ascent of man toward God without a tearing asunder.

THE ABANDONMENT at the supreme moment of the crucifixion, what an abyss of love on both sides!

God wears himself out through the infinite thickness of time and space in order to reach the soul and to captivate it. If it allows a pure and utter consent (though brief as a lightning flash) to be torn from it, then God conquers that soul. And when it has become entirely his, he abandons it. He leaves it completely alone, and it has in its turn, but gropingly, to cross the infinite thickness of time and space in search of him whom it loves. It is thus that the soul, starting from the opposite end, makes the same journey that God made toward it. And that is the cross.

39

Naked Pride

John Stott

THE ESSENCE OF SIN is man substituting himself for God, while the essence of salvation is God substituting himself for man. Man asserts himself against God and puts himself where only God deserves to be; God sacrifices himself for man and puts himself where only man deserves to be. Man claims prerogatives that belong to God alone; God accepts penalties which belong to man alone.

As we stand before the cross, we begin to gain a clear view both of God and of ourselves, especially in relation to each other. Instead of inflicting upon us the judgment we deserved, God in Christ endured it in our place. Hell is the only alternative. This is the "scandal," the stumbling-block, of the cross. For our proud hearts rebel against it. We cannot bear to acknowledge either the seriousness of our sin and guilt or our utter indebtedness to the cross. Surely, we say, there must be something we can do, or at least contribute, in order to make amends? If not, we often give the impression that we would rather suffer our own punishment than the humiliation of seeing God through Christ bear it in our place.

George Bernard Shaw, who had considerable insight into the subtleties of human pride, dramatized this in his comedy about the Salvation Army entitled *Major Barbara* (1905). Bill Walker, "a rough customer of about 25," arrives at the Army's West Ham shelter one cold January morning drunk and infuriated because his girlfriend Mog has not only been converted but "got another bloke." Bill's rival is Todger Fairmile, a champion music hall wrestler in Canning Town, who has also been converted. Accusing Jenny Hill, a young Salvation Army lass, of having set his girlfriend against him, Bill first seizes her by the hair until she screams and then strikes her with his fist in the face, cutting her lip. The bystanders mock him for his cowardice. He attacks a girl, they say, but he would not have the courage to hit Todger Fairmile. Gradually Bill's conscience and pride nag him, until he can no longer bear the insult. He determines to do something to redeem his reputation and expiate his guilt. He says in broad Cockney: "Aw'm gowin to Kennintahn, to spit in Todger Fairmawl's eye. Aw beshed Jenny Ill's fice; an nar Aw'll git me aown fice beshed. Ee'll itt me ardern Aw itt er. Thatll mike us square."

But Todger refuses to cooperate, so Bill returns shamefaced: "Aw did wot Aw said Aw'd do. Aw spit in is eye. E looks ap at the skoy and sez, 'Ow that Aw should be fahnd worthy to be spit upon for the gospel's sike!'…an Mog sez 'Glaory Allelloolier!'"

Jenny Hill says she is sorry and that he did not really hurt her, which makes him angrier still: "Aw downt want to be forgive be you, or be ennybody. Wot Aw did Aw'll py for. Aw trawd to gat me aown jawr browk to settisfaw you—"

Because that way has failed, however, he tries another ruse. He offers to pay a fine which one of his mates has just incurred, and produces a sovereign.

"Eahs the manney. Tike it; and lets ev no more o your fogivin and pryin an your Mijor jawrin me. Let wot Aw dan be dan an pide for; and let there be a end of it. This bloomin forgivin an neggin an jawrin mikes a menn thet sore that iz lawf's a burdn to im. Aw wownt ev it, Aw tell yer. Awve offered to py. Aw can do no more. Tike it or leave it. There it is," – and he throws the sovereign down.

The proud human heart is there revealed. We insist on paying for what we have done. We cannot stand the humiliation of acknowledging our bankruptcy and allowing somebody else to pay for us. The notion that this somebody else should be God himself is just too much to take. We would rather perish than repent, rather lose ourselves than humble ourselves.

Moreover, only the gospel demands such an abject self-humbling on our part. As Emil Brunner put it, "All other forms of religion – not to mention philosophy – deal with the problem of guilt apart from the intervention of God, and therefore they come to a 'cheap' conclusion. In them man is spared the final humiliation of knowing that the Mediator must bear the punishment instead of him. To this yoke he need not submit. He is not stripped absolutely naked."

But we cannot escape the embarrassment of standing stark naked before God. It is no use our trying to cover up like Adam and Eve in the garden. Our attempts at self-justification are as ineffectual as their fig-leaves. We have to acknowledge our nakedness, see the divine substitute wearing our filthy rags instead of us, and allow him to clothe us with his own righteousness. Nobody has ever put it better than Augustus Toplady in his immortal hymn "Rock of Ages":

> Nothing in my hand I bring,
> Simply to your Cross I cling;
> Naked, come to you for dress;
> Helpless, look to you for grace;
> Foul, I to the fountain fly;
> Wash me, Savior, or I die.

40

The Signature of Jesus

Brennan Manning

THERE IS A STORY of an old man who used to meditate early every morning under a big tree on the bank of the Ganges River. One morning, after he had finished his meditation, the old man opened his eyes and saw a scorpion floating helplessly in the water. As the scorpion was washed closer to the tree, the old man quickly stretched himself out on one of the long roots that branched out into the river and reached out to rescue the drowning creature. As soon as he touched it, the scorpion stung him. Instinctively the man withdrew his hand. A minute later, after he had regained his balance, he stretched himself out again on the roots to save the scorpion. This time the scorpion stung him so badly with its poisonous tail that his hand became swollen and bloody and his face contorted with pain.

At that moment, a passerby saw the old man stretched out on the roots struggling with the scorpion and shouted: "Hey, stupid old man, what's wrong with you? Only a fool would risk his life for the sake of an ugly, evil creature. Don't you know you could kill yourself trying to save that ungrateful scorpion?"

The old man turned his head. Looking into the stranger's eyes he said calmly, "My friend, just because it is the scorpion's nature to sting, that does not change my nature to save."

Sitting here at the typewriter in my study, I turn to the symbol of the crucified Christ on the wall to my left. And I hear Jesus praying for his murderers, "Father, forgive them. They do not know what they are doing."

The scorpion he had tried to save finally killed him. To the passerby, who sees him stretched out on the tree roots and who shouts, "Only a madman would risk his life for the sake of an ugly, ungrateful creature," I hear Jesus answer, "My friend, just because it is fallen mankind's nature to wound, that does not change my nature to save."

OVER A HUNDRED YEARS AGO in the Deep South, a phrase commonplace in our Christian culture today, *born again,* was seldom used. Rather, the words used to describe the breakthrough into a personal relationship with Jesus Christ were: "I was seized by the power of a great affection."

It was a profoundly moving way to indicate both the initiative of almighty God and the explosion within the human heart when Jesus becomes Lord. Seized by the power of a great affection was a visceral description of the phenomenon of Pentecost, authentic conversion, and the release of the Holy Spirit.

In March 1986 I was privileged to spend an afternoon with an Amish family in Lancaster, Pennsylvania. Jonas Zook, a widower, is eighty-two years old. His oldest daughter Barbara, 57, manages the household. The three other children, Rachel, 53, Elam, 47, and Sam, 45, are all severely retarded. When I arrived at noon with two friends, Joe and Kathy Anders, "little Elam"—about four feet tall, heavy-set, thickly bearded, and wearing the black Amish outfit with the circular hat—was coming out of the barn some fifty yards away. He had never laid eyes on me in his life, yet when he saw me step out of the car, he ran lickety-split in my direction. Two feet away, he threw himself into the air, wrapped his arms around my neck, his legs around my waist, and kissed me smack on the lips.

To say that I was stunned would be an understatement. But in the twinkling of an eye, Jesus set me free. I returned Elam's kiss. Then he jumped down, wrapped both his hands around my right arm, and led me on a tour of the farm. The Zooks raised piglets for a living.

A half-hour later at a lovely luncheon prepared by Barbara, Elam sat next to me. Midway through the meal, I turned around to say something to Joe Anders. Inadvertently, my right elbow slammed into Elam's rib cage. He did not wince; he did not groan. He wept like a child. His next move utterly undid me. Elam came to my chair and kissed me even harder on the lips. Then he kissed my eyes, my nose, my forehead, and cheeks. And there was Brennan, dazed, dumbstruck, weeping, seized by the power of a great affection. In his simplicity, Elam Zook was an icon of Jesus Christ. Why? Because his love for me did not stem from any attractiveness or lovability of mine. It was not conditioned by any response on my part. Elam loved me whether I was kind or unkind, pleasant or nasty. His love arose from a source outside of himself and myself.

Jesus came as the revealer of love. Jesus reveals God by being utterly transparent to him. What had been cloaked in mystery is clear in Jesus – that God is love. No man or woman has ever loved like Jesus Christ. Therein lies his divinity for me.

Jesus was seized by the power of a great affection and experienced the love of his Father in a way that burst all previous boundaries of understanding. And it is this Jesus, the wounded Jesus, who provides the final revelation of God's love. The crucified Christ is not an abstraction but the ultimate answer to how far love will go, what measure of rejection it will endure, how much selfishness and betrayal it will withstand. The uncon-ditional love of Jesus Christ nailed to the tree does not flinch before our perversity. "He took our sicknesses away and carried our diseases for us" (Matt. 8:17).

IN 1960, a pastor in East Germany wrote a play called *The Sign of Jonah*. The last scene dealt with the Final Judgment. All the peoples of the earth are assembled on the plain of Jehosaphat awaiting God's verdict.

They are not, however, waiting submissively; on the contrary, they are gathered in small groups, talking indignantly. One group is a band of Jews, a sect that has known little but religious, social, and political persecution throughout their history. Included in their number are victims of Nazi extermination camps. Huddled together, the group demands to know what right God has to pass judgment on them, especially a God who dwells eternally in the security of heaven.

Another group consists of American blacks. They too question the authority of God who has never experienced the misfortunes of men, never known the squalor and depths of human degradation to which they were subjected in the suffocating holds of slave ships. A third group is composed of persons born illegitimately, the butt all their lives of jokes and sneers.

Hundreds of such groups are scattered across the plain: the poor, the afflicted, the maltreated. Each group appoints a representative to stand before the throne of God and challenge his divine right to pass sentence on their immortal destinies. The representatives include a horribly twisted arthritic, a victim of Hiroshima, a blind mute. They meet in council and decide that this remote and distant God who has never experienced human agony is unqualified to sit in judgment unless he is willing to enter into the suffering, humiliated state of man and endure what they have undergone.

Their conclusion reads: You must be born a Jew; the circumstances of your birth must be questioned; you must be misunderstood by everyone, insulted and mocked by your enemies, betrayed by your friends; you must be persecuted, beaten, and finally murdered in a most public and humiliating fashion.

Such is the judgment passed on God by the assembly. The clamor rises to fever pitch as they await his response. Then a brilliant, dazzling light illuminates the entire plain. One by one those who have passed judgment on God fall silent. For emblazoned high in the heavens for the whole world to see is the signature of Jesus Christ with this inscription above it: *I have served my sentence.*

41

Life in the Blood

Toyohiko Kagawa & Sadhu Sundar Singh

In him we have redemption through his blood…

EPHESIANS 1:7

THE APOSTLE PAUL says that redemption is the work of making up for *loss*. He illustrates it by the blood circulation with its action of metabolism. There are those who say that because God is love, he could not allow punishment. But that is too easy. It is like saying that because God is love, when you put water into a bag with a hole in it, the hole in the bag won't matter! You must close up the hole!

Unless you fill up the hole, the bag won't hold water. You can't reveal the glory of God if you have a hole in your heart, no matter how much of God's glory you receive. It is Christ who fills up that egregious hole.

Blood circulation has the power to heal wounds. My child once got a bad bruise on his nose at a friend's house. I was anxious as to whether it would ever heal up, but while I was worrying about it, the blood cured it and made the nose-form as it had been before. I thought it marvelous. Crabs are like that. If one of the claws of a crab is torn off, the next year a new claw is sure to grow. A pig's hindparts if cut off will grow again fat and round.

Love creates the same pattern anew. It redeems the place that was lost. To the measure of its depths, the love of God can perfectly heal the holes of the past, and all its sins. It does not merely repair the damages of sin, but even transforms that which has been broken into perfect health, perfect working capacity. Peter's life illustrates that.

Blood has a strange power. It cleanses the body of impurities, draws away the pus from injured tissues and restores them. It even has the power of rebuilding tissues that have been destroyed. Blood has the power of controlling the development of any part of the body, a power which reaches into the future.

Thus with the soul as well as the body. The power of Christ's blood means the power of love! If blood can bring recovery to the sores of the body, love has the power to redeem the wounds of the personality. If blood has the power to restore broken-down tissues, love can make the wounded person whole again, until he becomes a child of God.

The action of blood is universal; it functions throughout the body, feeding the nerve tissues, the digestive organs, the bones, the muscles, and circulating throughout the whole system, having the power to restore any part of it. It is the same with love. Love is endowed with the power to redeem and heal throughout the past, present and future, every part of the whole. The supreme manifestation of that love is the blood which Christ shed on the cross. This love enables us to believe in the forgiveness of past sins and the healing of past offences. **TOYOHIKO KAGAWA**

GOD IS LOVE and forgives us freely. But God does even more than this. Forgiveness alone is not enough to release us from our sins. Complete release only comes when we are free from the urge to sin. It is completely possible for us to receive forgiveness and still die from the consequences of our sin. The Master came not only to announce our forgiveness, but also to deliver us from the disease of our sin, from its consequences and from death – to break the relentless cycle of sin and death.

Consider the man who suffered from a debilitating disease of the brain. At times it would cause him to act irrationally and unpredictably. Under the influence of one such attack, he unwittingly struck out and killed another man. At trial, he was sentenced to death. But when his relatives appealed for mercy and explained the medical reasons for his temporary insanity, the governor granted clemency and pardoned him. But before his friends and relatives reached the prison to share this good news, the man had died as a result of his illness. So he gained nothing from the governor's pardon. Quite apart from the pardon, he needed treatment for his disease. Only then might he have lived to enjoy his release.

It is treatment we need, not just forgiveness. In ancient times, religious law forbade people to drink the blood of animals or to eat certain foods. These customs undoubtedly arose from the belief that such foods caused certain illnesses or, perhaps, that they would foster some savage animal behavior. The Master has said, "My flesh is food indeed and my blood is drink indeed," for they provide spiritual health and life.

Once a young man fell over a cliff. By the time he was rescued he had lost so much blood that he was almost dead. His father rushed him to a doctor, but the doctor said: "He will certainly die, unless someone can be found who is willing to provide enough blood for a massive transfusion." Now the father's heart overflowed with such love for his son that he offered his own blood, though he knew it would cost him his own life. So by the sacrificial love of his father, the young man was given new life. We, too, have fallen headlong from the mountain of righteousness and lie broken and wounded by sin, with our life fast ebbing away. But if we turn to the Master, he freely gives us his spiritual blood so that we might be saved from death and regain life. Indeed, he came to us for this very purpose.

SADHU SUNDAR SINGH

42

The Central Murder

Dale Aukerman

THE PRAGMATIC READINESS to sacrifice human life, which found superlative expression through Caiaphas, took as focal victim Jesus of Nazareth. But there was something that outweighed that readiness, even its totality within all of history: The willingness of Jesus to become victim of that pragmatism and thus

> *identify himself* with the countless victims of wars, with all those who have been deliberately sacrificed to the Political Necessities and Social Duty, with the millions of human beings who have been slaughtered and constrained to slaughter each other by being more or less persuaded that their deaths would be serving Justice and Law. By his readiness to become the victim of such a belief, Jesus unmasked its monstrous falsity, and showed

his disciples in advance that they could never adopt it themselves (Jean Lasserre, *War and the Gospel*).

On a ruined wall in Hiroshima is dimly etched the figure of a human being who was standing next to it when the flash came. The body, though instantaneously vaporized, stopped enough of the awful light to leave that abiding epitaph. When German theologian Heinrich Vogel gazed at the dim silhouette, the thought gripped him: Jesus Christ was there in the inferno with that person; what was done to him was done to Christ; the horror he may have had no instant to feel, Jesus felt. The Light of the world stood uncomprehended, comprehending, and undone by the hideous splendor of humankind's stolen fire. God's son yielded to humanity's Little Boy (code name of that bomb). Jesus' presence in the midst of atomic holocaust was intimated also in the fact that the bomb on Nagasaki exploded very close to the largest Christian cathedral in all Asia, annihilating 1,100 worshippers.

We can envision the risen Jesus there at the foot of the cross of cloud, the victor as victim. But the death of the person next to the wall, the death of those Japanese multitudes, already impinged on Jesus at Skull Hill. What the crucified one took to himself at the midpoint

Dale Aukerman · 235

of history, the risen one, drawing near, takes to himself hour after hour, disease by disease, enmity by enmity, war by war in the sequence of history.

I can meditate on the vaporization of a few in Hiroshima and Nagasaki; but my mind cannot visualize the snuffing out of 250,000 human beings. There is, though, the slain One, whose mind, heart, body in A.D. 30 and A.D. 1945 took that in. Because the fullness of God dwelt in him, he could take to himself and register to the full the monstrous magnitudes of human hate, killing, and death.

What is currently being prepared for and what would be fought would come as war against all human beings, not just against those in "enemy" countries. All would be to some extent casualties of the war; quite possibly all would die, over a period of time, as its victims. In Hebrew thought a single murder cast its imperiling shadow over the entire faith community; the gravity of the disorder it constituted impinged on all who were within that corporateness. In that perspective, what an ominous hovering immensity hangs over us today because of private murders, the savor and stimulus of media violence, and military slaughters past, present, future. But that immensity in its greater breadth looms over all humanity in its corporateness—looms as non-material magnitude, which, for its full globe-encircling scope, has taken concretization in the nuclear arsenals. It is as the central person of all humanity that Jesus Christ is presently threatened by this guilt and doom which he earlier bore.

God, in order that we might meet him, narrowed himself down into Jesus. But Jesus was also the narrowing down of the totality of humankind. He was formed that our vision might rest not only on this focal expression of the invisible God but also on this singular image of the neighbors we have been too nearsighted to see and of the myriads of human beings we have no sight to see. This latter dimension is indicated by Jesus' words in the judgment scene pictured in Matthew 25:31–46. Though we cannot envision all who should be within our view, we are to see him who is focus and head of that vast throng.

That three hundred million persons or a billion or four billion might be killed in a nuclear world war is beyond the imagination of any mortal. My nearest approach to the magnitude of that horror comes when I realize that Jesus would be the central victim in the midst of the annihilation. Each victim he would know;

each passion, each death he would feel. He in whom God has drawn near would be there with the least of all who are his in a thousand infernos. The slain Brother would be there with every brother and sister, with every terrified child, as the slower ghastliness of radiation sickness spread across the continents. A darkness more enduring than that on a long-ago Passover would come across the world, after a more ominous quaking of earth and disintegration of rocks. From innumerable parched lips would come some echo of the cry, "My God, my God, why hast thou forsaken me?" For that elimination of intolerable neighbors would bring with it an apparent doing away with God. But the One who gave supreme utterance to that cry, the Neighbor-Brother-God, who was done away with, would be there in the midst.

This means that all the nuclear weapons delivery systems of this world are zeroed in on a target that comprehends all human targets: Jesus. Christians must understand that there is no aiming of nuclear weapons and no assent to them which does not zero in on him: "As you did it to one of the least of these my brethren, you did it to me."

Our Lord does not ask that we stare heroically into the nuclear abyss; he asks that we look toward him and let our sight become aligned with his. If we are to love as he has loved us, our perception of how he has loved focuses toward his earthly life and death, and yet takes in how he loves us all now. Will we love near and far neighbors as he now loves us? Will we see any who come within our vision as partly overshadowed by the pathos and peril of nuclear guilt and nuclear war? Will we put our lives on the line, his line, against the onrush of chaos?

43

Thirsting

Alexander Stuart Baillie

Later, knowing that all was now completed, and so that the Scripture would be fulfilled, Jesus said, "I thirst." **JOHN 19:28**

THE WORDS "I THIRST," literal as they are, spoken to meet a deep human need, become for us pregnant with new and deeper meaning in the spiritual sense. Their symbolism becomes real as we think of life. When we look out upon the bedraggled flock of humanity, sheep without a shepherd, we know that they have many thirsts. There are those who thirst for everything save righteousness. Their lives are so engrossed and encompassed within the limits of their world of time-space that they forget that there might be some other relations to life. Such crass limitations make life little and cramped. By shutting out the Eternal, they lose all that is truly worthwhile. They forget that life abundant is not to be found within their little cosmos of human desires.

We have seen people thirsting for wealth. So great was their thirst for the yellow metal that they were willing to sell their very souls to gain possession of it. They imagined that they would like to become a second King Midas, this without really thinking their ways through all the limited implications of the tragic final results. To such the words of Jesus come back and he says, "Life consists not in the abundance of things which one possesses."

There have been those who have thirsted for pleasure, for a life of thrills. Many have given themselves with singleness of purpose to this end, and have found it very unsatisfactory. Somewhere I read of an actress who had given herself to the pursuit of the flying phantom–pleasure. She tried all and then life began to grow weary and tiresome. Blasé and jaded, she gave up in despair. In her sad plight, she thought of one more thrill and that was through the gateway of death. So she arranged to commit suicide in as artistic a manner as possible, in order to make life yield its greatest and final thrill. Others may be like—was it Shelley?—who, after he rubbed cayenne pepper on his tongue, drank down a glass of cold sherry wine, saying, "O, for a life of sensations!"

Poets have expressed their feelings relative to a life of empty pleasure. One poet gave vent to his plaintive thoughts in the following words:

> I tried the broken cistern, Lord,
> But, Ah! the waters failed.
> E'en as I stooped to drink they fled
> And mocked me as I wailed.

Some have thirsted for rank and station. Their desire has been to get into the select circle. In order to do this they have been willing to compromise with their better selves in order to live a life of sham and outward show. Little does man know that in these pathetic plights of his, when he is trying to assuage his thirsts, his needs are deeper, far deeper than money, pleasure, rank or station. He needs God!

Our deep spiritual needs, which are thirsts, can be met by Christ. It is God's desire that every person should know the real joys of life. Augustine, the great churchman, expressed this idea as follows: "Thou hast made us for Thyself, and we cannot find rest until we find it in Thee." In other words, we cannot have our thirst satisfied until God does it for us.

This age needs to become more realistic. It needs to listen again to the words of Jesus, who said, "I thirst." He who is the Son of Man, the Son of God, is our example. He is the great pioneer in every realm of life. Surely if he thirsted, how much more do we? Humanity needs to get away from the world of "things as they are" into the world of "things as they ought to be." This means that men and women must learn to live for others. It is only when we can live a life of self-forgetfulness that we get our truest joy out of life. One needs to keep on thirsting because life grows and enlarges. It has no end; it goes on and on; it becomes more beautiful. When one has done his best there is, he finds, still more to learn and so much to do. He cannot be satisfied until he attains unto the stature of Jesus, unto a perfect man, and ever thirsts for God.

44

It Is Done

Watchman Nee

When he received the drink, Jesus said, "It is finished." With that, he bowed his head and gave up his spirit. **JOHN 19:30**

Good Friday is the day when you can do nothing. Bewailing and lamenting your manifold sins does not in itself make up for them. Scouring your soul in a frenzy of spring cleaning only sterilizes it; it does not give it life. On Good Friday, finally, we are all, mourners and mockers alike, reduced to the same impotence. Someone else is doing the terrible work that gives life to the world.
VIRGINIA STEM OWENS

CHRISTIANITY BEGINS not with a big *do*, but with a big *done*. We begin our Christian life by depending not upon our own doing but upon what Christ has done.

Until you realize this you are no Christian; for to say: "I can do nothing to save myself; but by his grace God *has done* everything for me in Christ," is to take the first step of faith.

If I put a dollar bill between the pages of a magazine, and then burn the magazine, where is the dollar bill? It has gone the same way as the magazine—to ashes. Where the one goes the other goes too. Their history has become one. But, just as effectively, God has put us in Christ. What happened to him happened also to us. All the experiences he met, we too have met *in him*. "Our old man was crucified with him, that the body of sin might be done away, that so we should no longer be in bondage to sin" (Rom. 6:6). That is not an exhortation to struggle. That is history: our history, written in Christ before we were born. Do you believe this? It is true! Our crucifixion with Christ is a glorious historic fact. Our deliverance from sin is based, not on what we can do, nor even on what God is going to do for us, but on what he has already done in Christ. When that fact dawns upon us and we rest back upon it (Rom. 6:11), then we have found the secret of a holy life.

But it is true that we know all too little of this in experience. Consider an example. If someone makes a very unkind remark about you in your presence, how do you meet the situation? You compress your lips, clench your teeth, swallow hard, and take a firm grip upon yourself; and if with a great effort you manage to suppress all sign of resentment and be reasonably polite in return, you feel you have gained a great victory. But the resentment is still there; it has merely been covered up. And at times you do not even succeed in covering it. What is the trouble? The trouble is that you are trying to walk before you have learned to sit, and that way lies sure defeat. Let me repeat: no Christian experience begins with walking, but always with a definite sitting down: "And God raised us up with Christ and seated us with him in the heavenly realms in Christ Jesus" (Eph. 2:6). The secret of deliverance from sin is not to *do* something but to rest on what God has done.

An engineer living in a large city in the West left his homeland for the Far East. He was away for two or three years, and during his absence his wife was unfaithful to him and went off with one of his best friends. On his return home he found he had lost his wife, his two children and his best friend.

At the close of a meeting that I was addressing, this grief-stricken man unburdened himself to me. "Day and night for two solid years my heart has been full of hatred," he said. "I am a Christian, and I know I ought to forgive my wife and my friend, but though I try and try to forgive them, I simply cannot. Every day I resolve to love them, and every day I fail. What can I do about it?" "Do nothing at all," I replied. "What do you mean?" he asked, startled. "Am I to continue to hate them?"

So I explained: "The solution of your problem lies here, that when the Lord Jesus died on the cross he not only bore your sins away but he bore *you* away too. When he was crucified, your old man was crucified in him, so that that unforgiving 'you,' who simply cannot love those who have wronged you, has been taken right out of the way in his death. God has dealt with the whole situation in the cross. Just say to him, 'Lord, I cannot love and I give up trying, but I count on Thy perfect love. I cannot forgive, but I trust Thee to forgive instead of me, and to do so henceforth in me.'"

The man sat there amazed and said, "That's all so new, I feel I must *do* something about it." Then a moment later he added again, "But what can I *do?*" "God is waiting till you cease to do," I said. "When you cease doing, then God will begin. Have you ever tried to save a drowning man? The trouble is that his fear prevents him from entrusting himself to you. When that is so, there are just two ways of going about it. Either you must knock him unconscious and then drag him to the shore, or else you must leave him to struggle and shout until his strength gives way before you go to his rescue. If you try to save him while he has any strength left, he will clutch at you in his terror and drag you under, and both he and you will be lost. God is waiting for your store of strength to be utterly exhausted before he can deliver you. Once you have ceased to struggle so hard, he will do everything. God is waiting for you to despair. He has done it all!"

And with radiant face he went off rejoicing.

45

The Father's Hands

George MacDonald

Jesus called out with a loud voice, "Father, into your hands I commit my spirit." When he had said this, he breathed his last.

LUKE 23:46

THE CRY, "Father, into your hands I commit my spirit," meant, "It is finished." Every highest human act is just a giving back to God of that which he first gave to us. "God, you have given me: here again is your gift. I send my spirit home." Every act of worship is a holding up to God of what God has made us. "Here, Lord, look what I have got: feel with me in what you have made me, in this your own bounty, my being. I am your child, and know not how to thank you save by uplifting the over-flowing of your life, and calling aloud, 'It is yours: it is

249

mine. I am yours, and therefore I am mine.'" The vast operations of the spiritual as of the physical world, are simply a turning again to the source.

The last act of our Lord in thus commending his spirit at the close of his life, was only a summing up of what he had been doing all his life. He had been offering this sacrifice, the sacrifice of himself, all the years, and in thus sacrificing he had lived the divine life. Every morning when he went out ere it was day, every evening when he lingered on the night-lapt mountain after his friends were gone, he was offering himself to his Father in the communion of loving words, of high thoughts, of speechless feelings; and, between, he turned to do the same thing in deed, namely, in loving word, in helping thought, in healing action toward his fellows. For the way to worship God while the daylight lasts is to work; the service of God, the only "divine service," is the helping of our fellows.

I do not seek to point out this commending of our spirits to the Father as a duty: that is to turn the highest privilege we possess into a burden grievous to be borne. But I want to show that it is the most simple and blessed in the human world.

For the Human Being may say thus with himself: "Am I going to sleep–to lose consciousness–to be helpless for a time–thoughtless–dead? Or, more awful consideration, in the dreams that may come may I not be weak of will and scant of conscience?–Father, into your hands I commit my spirit. I give myself back to you. Take me, soothe me, refresh me, make me over again. Am I going out into the business and turmoil of the day, where so many temptations may come to do less honorably, less faithfully, less kindly, less diligently than the Ideal Man would have me do? Father, into your hands. Am I going to do a good deed? Then, of all times, Father, into your hands, lest the enemy should have me now. Am I going to do a hard duty, from which I would gladly be turned aside–to refuse a friend's request, to urge a neighbor's conscience?–Father, into your hands I commit my spirit.

"Am I in pain? Is illness coming upon me to shut out the glad visions of a healthy brain, and bring me such as are troubled and untrue? Take my spirit, Lord, and see that it has no more to bear than it can bear. Am I going to die? Father, into your hands I commit my spirit. For it is your business, not mine. You will know every shade of my suffering; You will care for me with your perfect fatherhood. As a child I could bear great pain when my father was leaning over me, or had his arm about me: how much nearer my soul cannot your hands come! – yes, with a comfort, Father of me, that I have never yet even imagined; for how shall my imagination overtake your swift heart? I care not for the pain, so long as my spirit is strong, and into your hands I commit that spirit. If your love, which is better than life, receive it, then surely your tenderness will make it great."

46

A Cosmic Cross

Paul Tillich

*And Jesus cried again with a loud voice and yielded up his spirit.
And behold, the curtain of the temple was torn in two, from top
to bottom; and the earth shook, and the rocks were split; the
tombs also were opened, and many bodies of the saints who had
fallen asleep were raised, and coming out of their tombs after his
resurrection they went into the holy city and appeared to many.
When the centurion and those who were with him keeping watch
over Jesus saw the earthquake and what took place, they were
filled with awe and said, "Truly this was the son of God!"*

MATTHEW 27:50–54

IN THE STORIES of the crucifixion the agony and the
death of Jesus are connected with a group of events
in nature: Darkness covers the land; the curtain of

the temple is torn in two; the earth is shaken and the bodies of the saints rise out of their graves. Nature, with trembling, participates in the decisive event of history. The sun veils its head; the temple makes the gesture of mourning; the foundations of the earth are moved; the tombs are opened. Nature is in an uproar because something is happening which concerns the universe.

Since the time of the evangelists, wherever the story of Golgotha has been told as the turning event in the world-drama of salvation, the role nature played in this drama has also been told. Painters of the crucifixion have used all their artistic power to express the darkness over the land in almost unnatural colors. I remember my own earliest impression of Good Friday – the feeling of the mystery of the divine suffering, first of all, through the compassion of nature. And so did the centurion, the first pagan who witnessed for the Crucified. Filled with awe, with numinous dread, he understood in a naïve-profound way that something more had happened than the death of a holy and innocent man.

The sun veiled its face because of the depth of evil and shame it saw under the Cross. But the sun also veiled its face because its power over the world had ceased once and forever in these hours of its darkness.

The great shining and burning god of everything that lives on earth, the sun who was praised and feared and adored by innumerable human beings during thousands and thousands of years, had been deprived of its divine power when *one* human being, in ultimate agony, maintained His unity with that which is greater than the sun. Since those hours of darkness it is manifest that not the sun, but a suffering and struggling soul which cannot be broken by all the powers of the universe is the image of the Highest, and that the sun can only be praised in the way of St. Francis, who called it our brother, but not our god.

"The curtain of the temple was torn in two." The temple tore its gown as the mourners did because He, to whom the temple belonged more than to anybody else, was thrown out and killed by the servants of the temple. But the temple – and with it, all temples on earth – also complained of its own destiny. The curtain which made the temple a holy place, separated from other places, lost its separating power. He who was expelled as blaspheming the temple, had cleft the curtain and opened the temple for everybody, for every moment. *This* curtain cannot be mended anymore, although there are priests and ministers and pious people who try to mend it. They will *not* succeed because He, for whom every place was a sacred place, a place where God is present, has been hung upon the cross in the name of the holy place.

When the curtain of the temple was torn in two, God judged religion and rejected temples. After this moment temples and churches can only mean places of concentration on the holy which is the ground and meaning of every place. And like the temple, the earth was judged at Golgotha. Trembling and shaking, the earth participated in the agony of the man on the cross and in the despair of all those who had seen in him the beginning of the new eon. Trembling and shaking, the earth proved that it is not the motherly ground on which we can safely build our houses and cities, our cultures and religious systems. Trembling and shaking, the earth pointed to another ground on which the earth itself rests: the self-surrendering love on which all earthly powers and values concentrate their hostility and which they cannot conquer. Since the hour when Jesus uttered a loud cry and breathed his last and the rocks were split, the earth ceased to be the foundation of what we build on her. Only insofar as it has a deeper ground can it stand; only insofar as it is rooted in the same foundation in which the cross is rooted can it last.

And the earth not only ceases to be the solid ground of life; she also ceases to be the lasting cave of death. Resurrection is not something added to the death of him who is the Christ; but it is implied in his death, as the story of the resurrection before the resurrection, indicates. No longer is the universe subjected to the law of death out of birth. It is subjected to a higher law, to the law of life out of death by the death of him who represented eternal life. The tombs were opened and bodies were raised when one man in whom God was present without limit committed his spirit into his Father's hands. Since this moment the universe is no longer what it was; nature has received another meaning; history is transformed and you and I are no more, and should not be anymore, what we were before.

Resurrection

SEVEN STANZAS AT EASTER

John Updike

Make no mistake: if He rose at all
it was as His body;
if the cells' dissolution did not reverse, the molecules
    reknit, the amino acids rekindle,
the Church will fall.

It was not as the flowers,
each soft Spring recurrent;
it was not as His Spirit in the mouths and fuddled
    eyes of the eleven apostles;
it was as His flesh: ours.

The same hinged thumbs and toes,
the same valved heart
that – pierced – died, withered, paused, and then
    regathered out of enduring Might
new strength to enclose.

Let us not mock God with metaphor,
analogy, sidestepping, transcendence;
making of the event a parable, a sign painted in the
    faded credulity of earlier ages:
let us walk through the door.

The stone is rolled back, not papier-maché,
not a stone in a story,
but the vast rock of materiality that in the slow
    grinding of time will eclipse for each of us
the wide light of day.

And if we will have an angel at the tomb,
make it a real angel,
weighty with Max Planck's quanta, vivid with hair,
    opaque in the dawn light, robed in real linen
spun on a definite loom.

Let us not seek to make it less monstrous,
for our own convenience, our own sense of beauty,
lest, awakened in one unthinkable hour, we are
    embarrassed by the miracle,
and crushed by remonstrance.

47

The Strangest Story of All

C. S. Lewis

WE COME to the strangest story of all, the story of the Resurrection. It is very necessary to get the story clear. I heard a man say, "The importance of the Resurrection is that it gives evidence of survival, evidence that the human personality survives death." On that view what happened to Christ would be what had always happened to all men, the difference being that in Christ's case we were privileged to see it happening.

This is certainly not what the earliest Christian writers thought. Something perfectly new in the history of the Universe had happened. Christ had defeated death. The door which had always been locked had for the very first time been forced open. This is something quite distinct from mere ghost-survival. I don't

263

mean that they disbelieved in ghost-survival. On the contrary, they believed in it so firmly that, on more than one occasion, Christ had had to assure them that he was *not* a ghost. The point is that while believing in survival they yet regarded the Resurrection as something totally different and new.

The Resurrection narratives are not a picture of survival after death; they record how a totally new mode of being has arisen in the Universe. Something new had appeared in the Universe: as new as the first coming of organic life. This Man, after death, does not get divided into "ghost" and "corpse." A new mode of being has arisen. That is the story. What are we going to make of it?

The question is, I suppose, whether any hypothesis covers the facts so well as the Christian hypothesis. That hypothesis is that God has come down into the created universe, down to manhood—and come up again, pulling it up with him. The alternative hypothesis is not legend, nor exaggeration, nor the apparitions of a ghost. It is either lunacy or lies. Unless one can take the second alternative (and I can't) one turns to the Christian view.

"What are we going to make of Christ?" There is no question of what we can make of him, it is entirely a question of what he intends to make of us. You must accept or reject the story.

The things he says are very different from what any other teacher has said. Others say, "This is the truth about the Universe. This is the way you ought to go," but he says, "I am the Truth, and the Way, and the Life." He says, "No person can reach absolute reality, except through me. Try to retain your own life and you will be inevitably ruined. Give yourself away and you will be saved." He says, "If you are ashamed of me, if, when you hear this call, you turn the other way, I also will look the other way when I come again as God without disguise. If anything whatever is keeping you from God and from me, whatever it is, throw it away. If it is your eye, pull it out. If it is your hand, cut it off. If you put yourself first you will be last. Come to me everyone who is carrying a heavy load. I will set that right. Your sins, all of them, are wiped out, I can do that. I am Rebirth. I am Life. Eat me, drink me, I am your Food. And finally, do not be afraid, I have overcome the whole Universe." That is the issue.

48

Merry Easter?

Frederica Mathewes-Green

IT'S THAT TIME of year again, when school children are coloring pictures of Jesus hanging from a cross, and shop owners fill their windows with gaily colored cutouts of the Flogging at the Pillar. In the malls everyone's humming along with seasonal hits on the sound system, like "O Sacred Head, Sore Wounded" (did you hear the Chipmunks' version?). Car dealers are promoting Great Big Empty-Tomb Size discounts on Toyotas.

Yes, it's beginning to look a lot like Easter. Who hasn't been invited to an "In His Steps" party, where players move plastic pieces around a board emblazoned with a map of Jesus' last suffering day in Jerusalem?

Not me, for one. Somehow we just don't make the same boisterous fun of Holy Week that we do of Christmas. No one plans to have a holly jolly Easter.

Easter just isn't fun in the same way Christmas is, a type of fun that could be better described as styled for children. It's a commonplace to say that "Christmas is for children," but what about Easter? Is it for children, too?

It sure didn't seem so to me, back then. Compared to Christmas, Easter was boring. Chocolate bunnies: good. Scratchy new crinolines: bad. Long blah-blah-blah at church. A lot of wordy grown-up buildup leading to, it seemed, no payoff. You could always count on Christmas to change a lot of stuff, especially in the toybox. Easter didn't change anything.

But when you think about the astonishing claims Christians make for Easter, that neglect seems pretty strange, even to an outsider. My friend Mitch is Jewish, but his encounters with suffering during medical training led him to doubt whether there even is a God. Yet last Christmas he sent me this note:

> Looking at the Christmas thing as a man raised in a
> Jewish home, the big celebration in Christianity should

be Easter. No Easter, no Christianity. So all the focus on Christmas, at least to me, seems misdirected.

Why Christians don't whoop it up more at Easter is a mystery to me. How inspirational! How joyful! That is the time to toast each other, lay on gifts, attend worship services, pack in the rich food. Something really substantial and holy to remember.

No Easter, no Christianity. Mitch has a point. If Jesus didn't rise from the dead, who cares whether he was born in a manger or a 7-Eleven? If he didn't rise from the dead, Christmas is meaningless too.

I remember my toybox, but not much of what was in it, and I don't retain any of those thrilling Christmas toys today. When I grew up, I put away childish things. When I grew up I began to be concerned with bigger things, many of them difficult to comprehend. Like Mitch, I saw suffering and death. I saw people live through situations so crushingly unfair that it was impossible that the universe bore no witness, impossible that there was no God who could wipe tears away and effect justice on the last day. I saw people find within themselves nobility to overcome, as well, and heard them say the strength came from a source beyond their own.

These are not things children have to think about.

Easter tells us of something children can't understand, because it addresses things they don't yet have to know: the weariness of life, the pain, the profound loneliness and hovering fear of meaninglessness. Yet in the midst of this desolation we find Jesus, triumphant over death and still shockingly alive, present to us in ways we cannot understand, much less explain. In him we find vibrancy of life, and a firm compassion that does not deny our suffering but transforms and illuminates it. He is life itself. As life incarnate, he could not be held back by death.

"O Death, where is your sting? O Hell, where is your victory?" wrote St. John Chrysostom, in a fourth-century sermon still used in every Orthodox church on Pascha (our name for Easter).

> Christ is risen, and you are overthrown.
> Christ is risen, and the demons are fallen.
> Christ is risen, and the angels rejoice.
> Christ is risen, and life reigns.
> Christ is risen, and not one dead remains in the grave.

On Pascha we will sing, over and over, dozens of times, "Christ is risen from the dead, trampling down death by death, and upon those in the tombs bestowing life." It is not a children's song. But grown-ups are taller, and can see farther, and know what hard blows life can bring. Easter may seem boring to children, and it is blessedly unencumbered by the silly fun that plagues Christmas. Yet it contains the one thing needful for every human life: the good news of Resurrection.

Easter didn't change anything? Easter changes everything.

49

In the Light of Victory

Alister E. McGrath

THE RESURRECTION OF JESUS is a sign of God's purpose and power to restore his creation to its full stature and integrity. Just as death could be seen as the culmination of all that is wrong with the world, so the resurrection can be seen as a pledge of God's ultimate victory over the disorder which plagues his creation on account of the fall. Death is the greatest enemy, and yet death has been defeated by God through Christ. And so we are given hope that the remainder of the powers and forces that confront us are similarly being defeated and their power broken.

The cross spells freedom. It brings liberation from *false understandings of God*. It shows that God is *there* – despite all the suggestions that he is not. Good Friday seemed to confirm the idea that God was dead, asleep or indifferent. Easter Day showed that God was alive, well and caring. The cross frees us from the idea that human nature is somehow too sinful, or the human dilemma too complex, for God to do anything about it. The surly bonds which tie us to these deeply pessimistic and oppressive views of God are torn apart by the cross. The creator becomes a creature within his own creation, in order to recreate it. In the aftermath of Gethsemane, we catch the fragrance of Eden. Jesus was betrayed within the garden of Gethsemane, in order to undo the disobedience of human nature within the garden of Eden. The resurrection is like the first day of a new creation.

So how does this image of what God achieved through the cross help us make sense of sin? What does it tell us about our situation apart from Christ? It encourages us to think of sin as enslavement and oppression. That enslavement could be political, military or economic. It is like the oppression which burdened the Israelites in Egypt, and which so grievously affects many people in poorer nations today. It invites us to imagine the sense of despair and hopelessness which plagued the continent of Europe in the darker days of Nazi occupation.

It declares, "*This* is what sin is like." It reminds us that an objective state of oppression leads to a subjective feeling of oppression. No amount of tinkering around with the subjective side of things can ever change the real situation, which causes that sense of despair in the first place. Real peace of mind requires a real change in our situation.

Now think of the cross and resurrection of Jesus as breaking the power of sin. But if the power of sin, death and evil has been broken, how can we make sense of the fact that it still continues to plague us? Human history and Christian experience tell us of a constant struggle against sin and evil in our own lives, even as Christians. There is a real danger, it would seem, that talking about the "the victory of faith" will become nothing more than empty words, masking a contradiction between faith and experience. How can we handle this problem?

A helpful way of understanding this difficulty was developed by a group of distinguished writers, such as C. S. Lewis in England and Anders Nygren in Sweden. They noticed important parallels between the New Testament and the situation during the Second World War. The victory won over sin through the death of

Christ was like the liberation of an occupied country from Nazi rule. We need to allow our imaginations to take in the sinister and menacing idea of an occupying power. Life has to be lived under the shadow of this foreign presence. And part of the poignancy of the situation is its utter hopelessness. Nothing can be done about it. No one can defeat it.

Then comes the electrifying news. There has been a far-off battle. And somehow, it has turned the tide of the war. A new phase has developed, and the occupying power is in disarray. Its backbone has been broken. In the course of time, the Nazis will be driven out of every corner of Europe. But they are still present in the occupied country.

In one sense, the situation has not changed, but in another, more important sense, the situation has changed totally. The scent of victory and liberation is in the air. A total change in the psychological climate results. I remember once meeting a man who had been held prisoner in a Japanese prisoner-of-war camp in Singapore. He told me of the astonishing change in the camp atmosphere which came about when one of the prisoners (who owned a shortwave radio) learned of the collapse of the Japanese war effort in the middle of

1945. Although all in the camp still remained prisoners, they knew that their enemy had been beaten. It would only be a matter of time before they were released. And those prisoners, I was told, began to laugh and cry, as if they were free already.

The end of the Second World War in Europe came about a year after the establishment of the bridgeheads in Normandy in June 1944. But an objective change had taken place some time before in the theatre of war – with a resulting subjective change in the hearts and minds of captive people. And so with us now. In one sense, victory has not come; in another, it has. The resurrection declares in advance of the event God's total victory over all evil and oppressive forces – such as death, evil and sin. Their backbone has been broken, and we may begin to live *now* in the light of that victory, knowing that the long night of their oppression will end.

50

Paradise Now

Howard Hageman

Then he said, "Jesus, remember me when you come into your kingdom." Jesus answered him, "I tell you the truth, today you will be with me in paradise." **LUKE 23:42–43**

IT IS PERFECTLY AMAZING how we have made of the New Testament, no more than a small part of which deals with the future, something that has almost its chief relevance in the future, and not too certain a future at that. The crucified thief shared our way of thinking. Lord, remember me when thou comest into thy kingdom. No telling when that might be or when he thought it would be. But he did not expect it soon if for no other reason than that crucified daydreamers do not overnight become kings with kingdoms! It was the future – the distant future – which the penitent thief had in mind when he spoke.

But now again, look at the reply. "Today shalt thou be with me in paradise." What had been hoped for the future is here as a present possibility. You can, of course, reply that since both the thief and Jesus Christ were about to leave this life, it would have to be that very day that they were together in paradise. But this misses the point. Let me put it this way. If these same words had been spoken by our Lord to the penitent thief at a time and place when each of them still had fifty years to live, they would have meant the same. For these words do not refer so much to the place to which they were going, by virtue of their common death, as to the new relationship into which they had entered by reason of faith. "To be with me in paradise" is not primarily a promise for the future but a possibility for the present.

For to be with Jesus Christ, whenever and wherever it takes place, is to be in paradise. It is an experience that doubtless will become more perfect and complete when we have passed beyond the limitations of this mortal life. But that does not preclude its beginning here within the limitations of this mortal life. Heaven, as we call it, is not a totally distinct realm from earth into which we shall be translated by the fact of death. It is an experience that interpenetrates the experiences of our mortality. There is no heaven, no paradise possible in another world for those who have not begun, however imperfectly, their experience of it here.

The dying thief did not begin his experience of paradise after he had drawn his last breath in this world. He began it at the moment he recognized in his dying companion the Lord and Master of his life. And when his spirit left his body for that other world, it was simply to go on in greater realization of something which had already, though for a very short time, been begun here.

Now, lest you think I am spinning fancies and neglecting reality, let me hasten briefly to illustrate what I mean. I mean that it is possible even in the contradictions and confusions of this life to keep the center of your being calm and undisturbed. I mean that it is possible even in this life to go through one hellish situation after another with strength and confidence of spirit. I mean that it is possible to endure physical pain and suffering while the mind and heart are filled with peace and joy. That's what I mean by being in paradise even while you are still part of this earthly scene of chance and change.

And I know that it is life's most glorious possibility – possible only when we are there with Christ. It is his presence in our lives that makes paradise possible even on a cross. For, while I would be the last in the world to minimize those good things which God has prepared for them that love him, none of us needs to sit mooning and pining for their coming when the most heavenly possibilities are available to us right here and now.

Those who live victoriously, though they wait in great hope and expectation for the final triumph of God's grace, live even more in present experience of what that grace in Christ can do in their lives here and now. "Today shalt thou be with me in paradise" is no idle promise for an indefinite future but a simple statement of what Christ can and will do here and now if we put our trust in him and open our lives to his presence and his power.

And that, of course, is the tragedy and the glory of the penitent thief. His tragedy is that his introduction to paradise came so late. If only he had met our Lord two or three years earlier, what hell he might have been spared, from what defeats he would have been delivered, from what fears he would have been saved, what mistakes he would have avoided. And his glory is that he found him in time, not only to win eternity, but to gain strength of spirit and faith even in the agony of his cross.

His tragedy and his glory are not unlike yours and mine. And Good Friday is the opportunity to redeem tragedy into glory. For what is our tragedy but our failure to grasp what Christ can do for our lives here and now? And what is our glory but to discover with him how to live in heaven even while we are still on earth?

51

Impending Resurrection

Malcolm Muggeridge

We pay more attention to dying than to death. We're more concerned to get over the act of dying than to overcome death. Socrates mastered the art of dying; Christ overcame death as the last enemy. There is a real difference between the two things; the one is within the scope of human possibilities, the other means resurrection. It's not from ars moriendi, *the art of dying, but from the resurrection of Christ, that a new and purifying wind can blow through our present world. Here is the answer to Archimedes' challenge: "Give me somewhere to stand, and I will move the earth." If only a few people really believed that and acted on it in their daily lives, a great deal would be changed. To live in the light of resurrection—that is what Easter means.*

DIETRICH BONHOEFFER

JESUS AUDACIOUSLY abolished death, transforming it from a door that slammed to, into one that opened to whoever knocked. He made death, as Bonhoeffer joyously said on his way to be executed, for a Christian a beginning, not an end. It was the key to life; to die was to live.

This was what so impressed Tolstoy in the Christian concept of dying. Furthermore, Tolstoy observed that, whereas he and the tiny intellectual élite to which he belonged were horrified by the prospect of dying because they had seen no point in living, his peasants confronted death with equanimity, well content that their days should end, and serenely confident that their further existence, whatever shape it might have, would be part of God's loving purpose for them. His own despair at the prospect of the obliteration of his clamant ego was so overwhelming that he had to hide away a rope hanging in his study for fear of hanging himself with it. It was then that he turned back to the Gospels, and as Jesus spoke to him through their pages, the dark menacing figure of death was transformed into the shining promise of life, now in this world, and thereafter.

In our post-Christian era death has recovered its old terrors, becoming unmentionable, as sex has become ever more mentionable. Private parts are public, but death is our dirty little secret. What is more, the fantasy is sustained that as science has facilitated fornication without procreation, in due course it will facilitate life without death, and enable the process of extending our life span to go on and on for ever, so that it never does come to an end.

Thus Dr. Christiaan Barnard's heart-transplant operations, which caused so much excitement at the time, seemed to hold out the hope of replacing our parts as they wore out, and thus of keeping us on the road indefinitely, like old vintage cars. New hearts, kidneys, genitals, brain-boxes even, installed as and when required, the requisite spare-parts being taken from the newly dead, or maybe from mental defectives and other afflicted persons who might be said for one reason or another to be making no good use of them. The resultant immortal beings would have no occasion to be raised from the dead as Lazarus was. Nor would Jesus' wonderful words about being the resurrection and the life have any significance. For them, there was no dying, and therefore no rising from the dead. Nor will those who dream of living without dying be attracted by, or even comprehend, the notion of dying in order to live.

As I approach my own end, which cannot now be long delayed, I find Jesus' outrageous claim to be, himself, the resurrection and the life, ever more captivating and meaningful. Quite often, waking up in the night as the old do, and feeling myself to be half out of my body, so that it is a mere chance whether I go back into it to live through another day, or fully disengage and make off; hovering thus between life and death, seeing our dear earth with its scents and sounds and colors, as I have known and loved them, more, perhaps, as Bernanos said, than I have dared to admit; recalling the golden hours of human love and human work, at the same time vouchsafed a glimpse of what lies ahead, Eternity rising in the distance, a great expanse of ineffable light—so placed, I hear Jesus' words ring triumphantly through the universe, spanning my two existences, the one in Time drawing to a close and the one in Eternity at its glorious beginning. So at last I may understand, and understanding, believe; see my ancient carcass, prone between the sheets, stained and worn like a scrap of paper dropped in the gutter, muddy and marred with being trodden underfoot, and, hovering over it, myself, like a butterfly released from its chrysalis stage and ready to fly away. Are caterpillars told of their impending resurrection? How in dying they will be transformed from poor earth-crawlers into creatures of the air, with exquisitely painted wings? If told, do they believe? Is it conceivable to them that so constricted an existence as theirs should burgeon into so gay and lightsome a one as a butterfly's? I imagine the wise old caterpillars shaking their heads—no, it can't be; it's a fantasy, self-deception, a dream. Similarly, our wise ones. Yet in the limbo between living and dying, as the night clocks tick remorselessly on, and the black sky implacably shows not one single streak or scratch of gray, I hear those words: *I am the resurrection and the life*, and feel myself to be carried along on a great tide of joy and peace.

52

The End Is Life

Frederick Buechner

Next day, that is, after the day of Preparation, the chief priests and the Pharisees gathered before Pilate and said, "Sir, we remember how that impostor said, while he was still alive, 'After three days I will rise again.' Therefore order the sepulchre to be made secure until the third day, lest his disciples go and steal him away and tell the people, 'He has risen from the dead,' and the last fraud will be worse than the first." Pilate said to them, "You have a guard of soldiers; go, make it as secure as you can." So they went and made the sepulchre secure by sealing the stone and setting a guard. **MATTHEW 27:62–66**

OF ALL THE GREAT PAINTERS of the world, the one that I would choose to paint this scene is Rembrandt. I would want it done in chiaroscuro, in terms of light and shade, with the chamber where Pilate receives the delegation almost entirely in shadow and with the light coming mainly from the faces themselves, especially the bearded faces of the Jewish elders, the creased faces of these pious old men as they lean a little too intensely forward to hear the Roman's answer. What will he say?

Then the helpless, old-man look when they are not quite sure that they have heard correctly as Pilate tells them in effect to do whatever they want to do. They have their own Temple guard, after all. "Make it as secure as you can," he tells them. This is precisely the moment for Rembrandt to paint: the venerable old men turning toward each other now, their faded old eyes wide with bewilderment, their mouths hanging loose – the kind of dazed, tremulous fear of old men suddenly called upon to do a young man's job. You are not sure whether to laugh or to cry. "As secure as you can," the Procurator of Judea tells them. But how secure is that? Their lips move, but no sound comes. God knows they have good reason to be afraid.

God knows. I think that we can say they have two reasons for being afraid, although they mentioned only one to Pilate, namely, that the dead man's disciples may, in the words of Matthew, "go and steal him away and tell the people..." So their spoken fear is the fear of a religious hoax.

But beneath the fear that they spoke about to Pilate lay another fear that they had not spoken about to anyone probably, not even to each other. This was the fear which I doubt very much if any one of them had had the courage to face more than fleetingly even within the secrecy of his own heart – the fear that the man whom they had crucified would *really* come alive again as he had promised, that the body that now lay dead in its tomb, disfigured by the mutilations of the cross, that this body or some new and terrible version of it would start to breathe again, stand up in its grave clothes and move toward them with unspeakable power. To the extent that deep within themselves the Jewish elders feared this as a real possibility, their being told by Pilate to make things as secure as they could was to have the very earth pulled out from under them. How does an old man keep the sun from rising? How do soldiers secure the world against miracles?

Yet maybe it is not as hard as they feared. I suspect that many of us could have greatly reassured them. I suspect that many of us could tell that all in all there is a lot one can do in defense against miracle, and, unless I badly miss my guess, there are thousands upon thousands of ministers doing precisely that at any given instant—making it as secure as they can, that is, which is really quite secure indeed.

The technique of the chief priests and the Pharisees was to seal the tomb with a boulder and then to post a troop of guards to keep watch over it; but even for its time that was crude. The point is not to try to prevent the thing from happening—like trying to stop the wind with a machine gun—but, every time it happens, somehow to explain it away, to deflect it, defuse it, in one way or another to dispose of it. And there are at least as many ways of doing this as there are sermons preached on Easter Sunday.

We can say that the story of the resurrection means simply that the teachings of Jesus are immortal like the plays of Shakespeare or the music of Beethoven and that their wisdom and truth will live on forever. Or we can say that the resurrection means that the spirit of Jesus is undying, that he himself lives on among us, the way that Socrates does, for instance, in the good that he left behind him, in the lives of all who follow his great example. Or we can say that the language in which the Gospels describe the resurrection of Jesus is the language of poetry.

But there is no poetry about it. Instead, it is simply proclaimed as a fact. *Christ is risen!* In fact, the very existence of the New Testament itself proclaims it. Unless something very real indeed took place on that strange, confused morning, there would be no New Testament, no Church, no Christianity.

Unlike the chief priests and the Pharisees, who tried with soldiers and a great stone to make themselves as secure as they could against the terrible possibility of Christ's really rising again from the dead, we are considerably more subtle. We tend in our age to say, "Of course, it was bound to happen. Nothing could stop it." But when we are pressed to say what it was that actually did happen, what we are apt to come out with is something pretty meager: this "miracle" of truth that never dies, the "miracle" of a life so beautiful that two thousand years have left the memory of it undimmed, the "miracle" of doubt turning into faith, fear into hope.

If I thought that when you strip it right down to the bone, this whole religion business is really just an affirmation of the human spirit, an affirmation of moral values, an affirmation of Jesus of Nazareth as the Great Exemplar of all time and no more, then like Pilate I would wash my hands of it. The human spirit just does not impress me that much, I am afraid. And I have never been able to get very excited one way or the other about moral values. And when I have the feeling that someone is trying to set me a good example, I start edging toward the door.

So what do I believe actually happened that morning on the third day after he died?

I can tell you this: that what I believe happened and what in faith and with great joy I proclaim, is that he somehow *got up*, with life in him again, and the glory upon him. And I speak very plainly here, very unfancifully. He got up. He said, "Don't be afraid." Rich man, poor man, child; sick man, dying; man who cannot believe, scared sick man, lost one. Young man with your life ahead of you. "Don't be afraid."

He said, "Feed my sheep," which is why, like the chief priests and the Pharisees, we try to make that tomb as secure as we can. Because this is what he always says: "Feed my sheep...my lambs." And this is what we would make ourselves secure from, knowing the terrible needs of the lambs and our abundance, knowing our own terrible needs.

He said, "Lo, I am with you always, even unto the end of the world."

Anxiety and fear are what we know best in this fantastic century of ours. Wars and rumors of wars. From civilization itself to what seemed the most unalterable values of the past, everything is threatened or already in ruins. We have heard so much tragic news that when the news is good we cannot hear it.

But the proclamation of Easter Day is that all is well. And as a Christian, I say this not with the easy optimism of one who has never known a time when all was not well but as one who has faced the cross in all its obscenity as well as in all its glory, who has known one way or another what it is like to live separated from God. In the end, his will, not ours, is done. Love is the victor. Death is not the end. The end is life. His life and our lives through him, in him. Existence has greater depths of beauty, mystery, and benediction than the wildest visionary has ever dared to dream. Christ our Lord has risen.

53

The Greatest Drama

Dorothy Sayers

CHRISTIANITY IS, OF COURSE, not the only religion that has found the best explanation of human life in the idea of an incarnate and suffering god. We might, therefore, prefer not to take this tale too seriously – there are disquieting points about it. Here we had a man of divine character walking and talking among us – and what did we find to do with him? The common people, indeed, "heard him gladly"; but our leading authorities in Church and State considered that he talked too much and uttered too many disconcerting truths. So we bribed one of his friends to hand him over quietly to the police, and we tried him on a rather vague charge of creating a disturbance, and had him publicly flogged and hanged on the common gallows, "thanking God we were rid of a knave." All this was not very creditable to us, even if he was (as many people thought and think) only a harmless crazy preacher. But if the Church is right about him, it was more discreditable still; for the man we hanged was God Almighty.

So that is the outline of the official story—the tale of the time when God was the underdog and got beaten, when he submitted to the conditions he had laid down and became a man like the men he had made, and the men he had made broke him and killed him. This is the dogma we find so dull—this terrifying drama of which God is the victim and hero.

If this is dull, then what, in Heaven's name, is worthy to be called exciting? The people who hanged Christ never, to do them justice, accused him of being a bore – on the contrary; they thought him too dynamic to be safe. It has been left for later generations to muffle up that shattering personality and surround him with an atmosphere of tedium. We have very efficiently pared the claws of the Lion of Judah, certified him "meek and mild," and recommended him as a fitting household pet for pale curates and pious old ladies.

To those who knew him, however, he in no way suggested a milk-and-water person; *they* objected to him as a dangerous firebrand. True, he was tender to the unfortunate, patient with honest inquirers and humble before Heaven; but he insulted respectable clergymen by calling them hypocrites; he referred to King Herod as "that fox"; he went to parties in disreputable company and was looked upon as a "gluttonous man and a wine-bibber, a friend of publicans and sinners"; he assaulted indignant tradesmen and threw them and their belong-ings out of the Temple; he drove a coach-and-horses through a number of sacrosanct and hoary regulations; he cured diseases by any means that came handy, with a shocking casualness in the matter of other people's pigs and property; he showed no proper deference for wealth or social position; when confronted with neat dialectical traps, he displayed a paradoxical humor that affronted serious-minded people, and he retorted by asking disagreeably searching questions that could not be answered by rule of thumb. He was emphati-cally not a dull man in his human lifetime, and if he was God, there can be nothing dull about God either. But he had "a daily beauty in his life that made us ugly," and officialdom felt that the established order of things would be more secure without him. So they did away with God in the name of peace and quietness.

Dorothy Sayers · 295

"*And the third day he rose again*"; what are we to make of that? One thing is certain: if he was God and nothing else, his immortality means nothing to us; if he was man and no more, his death is no more important than yours or mine. But if he really was both God and man, then when the man Jesus died, God died too, and when the God Jesus rose from the dead, man rose too, because they were one and the same person. The Church binds us to no theory about the exact composition of Christ's Resurrection Body. A body of some kind there had to be, since man cannot perceive the Infinite otherwise than in terms of space and time. It may have been made from the same elements as the body that disappeared so strangely from the guarded tomb, but it was not that old, limited, mortal body, though it was recognizably like it. In any case, those who saw the risen Christ remained persuaded that life was worth living and death a triviality—an attitude curiously unlike that of the modern defeatist, who is firmly persuaded that life is a disaster and death (rather inconsistently) a major catastrophe.

Now, nobody is compelled to believe a single word of this remarkable story. God (says the Church) has created us perfectly free to disbelieve in him as much as we choose. If we do disbelieve, then he and we must take the consequences in a world ruled by cause and effect.

Now, we may call this story exhilarating or we may call it devastating; we may call it revelation or we may call it rubbish; but if we call it dull, then words have no meaning at all. That God should play the tyrant over man is a dismal story of unrelieved oppression; that man should play the tyrant over man is the usual dreary record of human futility; but that man should play the tyrant over God and find him a better man than himself is an astonishing drama indeed. Any journalist, hearing of it for the first time, would recognize it as News; those who did hear it for the first time actually called it News, and good news at that; though we are apt to forget that the word Gospel ever meant anything so sensational.

Perhaps the drama is played out now, and Jesus is safely dead and buried. Perhaps. It is ironical and entertaining to consider that once at least in the world's history those words might have been spoken with complete conviction, and that was upon the eve of the Resurrection.

54

Threatened by Resurrection

Karl Barth

THE ESSENCE OF EASTER IS: Jesus is victor! Jesus – is it not he who was born in humblest lowliness, who died on the cross crying the cry of a derelict of God, he who forgave sins but who collapsed under the burden of sin, he, the humble, smitten by his fate; and of all those laden with grief, is he not the most burdened man of Nazareth? And he is to be *victor?*

Yes, it is a difficult, a dark truth, a word that scarcely can be tolerated by our ears – that word "resurrection." Not that it is hazy – its meaning is only too clear. It means what it says: something mighty, crystal-clear, complete. It signifies: That is the world, that is life with its imprisonments and tragedies of sorrow and of sin, life with its doubts and unanswered questions, life with its grave-mounds and crosses for the dead: a unique enigma, so immense that all answers are silent before it.

Nothing, absolutely nothing, can one do who is fated to this life of sin and death, with its thousand-fold festering needs; nothing can one do to amend it; nothing fills up this vacuum. Admit it; there is no way out! Unless it is the possibility of a miracle happening – no, not *a* miracle, but *the* miracle, the miracle of God – God's incomprehensible, saving intervention and mercy, the all-inclusive renewal that leads from death to life that comes from him, God's life-word, resurrection from the dead!

Resurrection – not progress, not evolution, not enlightenment, but a call from heaven to us: "Rise up! You are dead, but I will give you life." That is what is proclaimed here, and it is the only way that the world can be saved. Take away this summons, and make something else of it, something smaller, less than the absolute ultimate, or less than the absolutely powerful, and you have taken away all, the unique, the last hope there is for us on earth.

We do not like to see that we are deeply imprisoned, and that we absolutely cannot in any way help ourselves; that we are a people who live in the shadow and darkness of death; that this is proclaimed to us in the word "resurrection"—oh, that is for us the bitter, unendurable truth which stirs us to rebellion. That is the darkness in the clear word "resurrection."

Nevertheless, wherever that crystal-clear word "resurrection" shall be heard and understood, a prior word must be heard and perceived: "Death." It must be seen that in the midst of life, even in blooming and healthy life, there is a yawning chasm, a deep pit that cannot be filled by any art or power of man. Only one word is sufficient to cover this chasm, to fill this pit: "Jesus is victor!"—that is, "resurrection."

We must realize that all the paths of life upon which we walk are the same, now or at any later time, in that they all lead to the edge of the precipice. We cannot bridge this precipice but its bridging has been made manifest in the resurrection of Jesus Christ from the dead. Who would partake in this resurrection must first have seen this chasm, have discovered this pit.

And life is not easy; on the contrary, it becomes deadly earnest and difficult wherever this word "resurrection" resounds. Resurrection proclaims true freedom to us and lets us painfully discover our prison chains. It tells us that the one and only refuge is God. But it tells us that only because it shows us that all our positions on life's battlefield are lost and that we must vacate them. Against this fact we try to defend ourselves. We do not tolerate this pronouncement upon our lives, inherent in the resurrection proclamation. For that reason we deny the resurrection, or we at least minimize it. We alter it into something human.

And then, in our preaching on Easter Day, we say something about the rejuvenation of nature, or the romantic reappearing of the blossoms, or the revival of the frozen torpid meadows. We interpret the message that Jesus is victor, not in its literal sense, but we interpret it as a symbol or a human idea. In that case the message tells us that the world is not so bad off. After each and all evils there naturally follows something good. One must hope, and not lose courage!

We may be satisfied with this sort of resurrection. We may get along very well for some time with the comfort that death is not so terrible: "One must just not lose one's courage!" We may be satisfied for a long time with the romantic reappearing of the blossoms and the rejuvenation of spring, and thus forget the bitterness of present reality. It may be that, even as we stand beside the graves of loved ones, we find contentment in the thought of a spiritual continuation of this life. But the remarkable thing about it is that the real truth of the resurrection seems to be too strong for us, because it will not suffer itself to be hidden or concealed in these harmless clothes. It always breaks forth; it rises up and shouts at us, asking: "Do you really think that is all I have to say to you? Do you really believe that is why Jesus came to earth, why he agonized and suffered, why he was crucified and rose again on the third day, to become merely a symbol for the truth—which really is no truth—that eventually everything will be all right?"

No cultural education, no art, no evolutionary development helps us beyond our sins. We must receive assistance from the ground up. Then the steep walls of our security are broken to bits, and we are forced to become humble, poor, pleading. Thus we are driven more and more to surrender and give up all that we have, surrender and give up those things which we formerly used to protect and defend and hold to ourselves against the voice of the resurrection's truth.

55

Fear Not

Walter J. Ciszek

FACING A FIRING SQUAD is a pretty good test, I guess, of your theology of death. I didn't exactly pass the test with flying colors. Perhaps it all just happened too quickly, without any warning. There had been a revolt of the prisoners at Camp 5 in Norilsk, and when troops were called in to put down the revolt they divided the prisoners up into small groups and marched them off. I was rounded up in a group of thirty, one of the first groups herded out of the camp and led down to a sandpit about a mile away. We had no idea what disciplinary measures would be taken against us, but we never for a moment thought we would see the soldiers line up five yards in front of us with rifles ready, waiting only for the command to shoot. The command was given, the rifles raised, cocked on another command, and leveled at our heads. For a moment, as if in a dream, none of us really understood what was happening. Then the realization that we were actually looking into gun barrels awaiting only the command to fire came crashing into my consciousness with a force that stopped everything. My stomach turned once and went numb; my heart stopped; I'm sure I forgot to breathe; I couldn't move a muscle in my body; my mind went blank.

The first thought I actually remember thinking was a question: "Is this the end, Lord?" I know I started the act of contrition, but I remember the sensation of realizing that another part of me could not understand the words I was mumbling. The other part of me focused on the fact that in a fraction of a second I would stand before God, dumbfounded and unprepared, unable in the suddenness of my confusion and total terror to feel sorry for my sins, numbed into absolute inactivity, unable so much as to elicit a simple act of faith in the God I had learned to trust implicitly in every action of every day, let alone think with anticipation of meeting him face to face at last.

I can still remember vividly my awareness of the moment, and the second fear that gripped me, when

I realized I was incapable of performing any Christian act to redeem myself, paralyzed and terrified and yet conscious of what I should be doing—indeed was trying to do by rotely reciting the act of contrition without comprehension or meaning—in the last moment of life left to me before the veil parted and I would stand before God.

I have no idea how long that one moment lasted. Suddenly there was a shot in the distance, shouts, and a group of officers dashed out to stop our execution. All I know is that when the moment passed, my heart was pounding, every nerve and muscle shaking, my knees weak and trembling, my mind once again able to follow the sequence of events in a coherent way.

When we were finally marched off again, I tried to figure out what had happened to me.

Often enough, during the years of prison, of interrogations, of life in the camps, I had lived with the thought of death. On more than one occasion, I had been told I would be shot and I knew those threats were truly meant. I had seen men die around me of starvation, or illness, or sometimes just out of a lack of wanting to live any longer. I had faced death in my mind time and time again, had helped others in their final moments, had lived with the talk and presence of death. I had thought about it and reflected on it, had no fear of it, sometimes looked forward to it. What was there, then, about this moment that so terrified me, so completely unstrung me and made me incapable of functioning, of praying, even of thinking? Was it just the suddenness, the surprise, that had betrayed me?

That had to be part of it. Then, too, there was the physical fear. Everyone, sometime in his life, has experienced the effects of a sudden fright, a bad scare—a close call in an accident, perhaps, or an unexpected fall, maybe just a sudden, loud, strange noise. Animal instinct takes over at such moments; the mind goes blank, the body reacts: muscles tense, the heart quickens, the stomach tightens, nerves tingle. And when the moment passes, if it passes without physical contact or bodily harm, a reaction sets in as the body grows limp. Those are simply the physical signs of fear, and it is not surprising that the body should fear injury or even death. I cannot be sure—perhaps I will never know for certain until the moment of death approaches again—but I suspect that most of my panic before the firing squad in that sandpit outside Norilsk was due to such animal instinct in the face of a sudden and totally unexpected physical danger.

For the thought of death itself does not terrify me, had not terrified me all through the war, or prison, or the prison camps. Death must come to everyone at the end of this earthly life, but it is not therefore an absolute evil. If the good news of Christianity is anything, it is this: that death has no hidden terror, has no mystery, is not something we must fear. It is not the end of life, of the soul, of the person. Christ's death on Calvary was not in itself the central act of salvation, but his death and resurrection; it was the resurrection that completed his victory over sin and death, the heritage of humankind's original sin that made a Redeemer and redemption necessary. This was the "good news" of salvation, meant to remove our last doubts, last fears, about the nature of death.

For the resurrection was a fact, a fact as certain and as sure as death itself, and it meant that death held no victory over men, that life beyond death is a certainty and not just a human hope or fable. This was the fact that made new men of his once fearful disciples, this was the "good news" they preached. The little sermons recorded in the Acts of the Apostles center on this theme: God has raised Christ up from the dead, he has risen, and of that fact we are witnesses.

From the fall of Adam, God had promised a Redeemer. From the day death came into the world, God has promised a conqueror of death. And the good news to be preached throughout the world was that the Redeemer had come, death had been conquered! This is the joy of Easter, this is the peace it brings. "O foolish and slow of heart to believe," he said to the two disciples on their way to Emmaus, "ought not the Christ to have suffered these things, and so entered into his glory?" The victory of God's "anointed one," the Messiah, was to be over the "kingdom" of death and of sin, but how could he triumph unless he first suffered death and then broke its chains? Easter was the victory, Easter was the "good news." The peace of Easter is the peace that comes from knowing that the thing men had feared most – the end of life, annihilation, death – really holds no fear at all.

That is not a Christian fable; it is a fact, and the proof of it is the resurrection. "If Christ be not risen," said St. Paul to his Christians, "then your faith is in vain." You cannot be a Christian and doubt that fact.

Christ's coming upon earth, his taking on of human flesh, had no purpose if it was not to die and then to triumph over death. People had lived in expectation of his coming and his victory over death, until at last he came; since then, the "good news" of his victory over death has been proclaimed everywhere and has sustained in peace and joy those who have believed.

56

Waiting for Judas

Madeleine L'Engle

JOHN SAYS, "For God so loved the world that he gave his one and only Son, that whoever believes in him shall not perish but have eternal life. For God did not send his Son into the world to condemn the world, but to save the world through him."

When the world rejected that love and crucified it, Jesus did not lash back; he cried out in love and forgiveness.

Things are never quite the way they seem: things do not look the way we think they ought to look. Isaiah's description of Christ as the Suffering Servant bears little resemblance to the pretty young man with the beautifully combed beard and melancholy eyes we so often see depicted. But Isaiah's description rings much more true. In his own day, Jesus was a monster to many, disconcerting them with his unpredictability and the company he kept, vanishing to go apart to pray and to be alone with his Father just when people thought they needed him.

Perhaps if we are brave enough to accept our monsters, to love them, to kiss them, we will find that we are touching not the terrible dragon that we feared, but the loving Lord of all Creation.

And when we meet our Creator, we will be judged for all our turnings away, all our inhumanity to each other, but it will be the judgment of inexorable love, and in the end we will know the mercy of God which is beyond all comprehension. And we will know, as Hosea knew, that the heavenly Spouse says, "I will betroth you to me forever; I will betroth you in righteousness and justice, in love and compassion."

It is too good to believe; it is too strong, so we turn away, and the church leaves the Song of Songs out of the lectionary. But we can put it back in.

To the ancient Hebrew the love of God for his chosen people transcended the erotic love of man and woman. For the early Christian, it was the love of Christ for the church. For all of us it is the longing love of God for his

Creation, a love which is too strong for many of us to accept.

There is an old legend that after his death Judas found himself at the bottom of a deep and slimy pit. For thousands of years he wept his repentance, and when the tears were finally spent he looked up and saw, way, way up, a tiny glimmer of light. After he had contemplated it for another thousand years or so, he began to try to climb up towards it. The walls of the pit were dank and slimy, and he kept slipping back down. Finally, after great effort, he neared the top, and then he slipped and fell all the way back down. It took him many years to recover, all the time weeping bitter tears of grief and repentance, and then he started to climb up again. After many more falls and efforts and failures he reached the top and dragged himself into an upper room with twelve people seated around a table. "We've been waiting for you, Judas," Jesus said. "We couldn't begin till you came."

I heard my son-in-law, Alan, tell this story at a clergy conference. The story moved me deeply. I was even more deeply struck when I discovered that it was a story that offended many of the priests and ministers there. I was horrified at their offense. Would they find me, too, unforgivable?

But God, the Good Book tells us, is no respecter of persons, and the happy ending isn't promised to an exclusive club. It isn't—face it—only for Baptists, or Presbyterians, or Episcopalians. What God began, God will not abandon. *He who began a good work in you will carry it on to completion.* God loves *everyone*, sings the psalmist. What God has named will live forever, Alleluja!

The happy ending has never been easy to believe in. After the Crucifixion the defeated little band of disciples had no hope, no expectation of Resurrection. Everything they believed in had died on the cross with Jesus. The world was right, and they had been wrong. Even when the women told the disciples that Jesus had left the stone-sealed tomb, the disciples found it nearly impossible to believe that it was not all over. The truth was, it was just beginning.

57

The Mystery of the Poor

Dorothy Day

ON HOLY THURSDAY, truly a joyful day, I was sitting at the supper table at St. Joseph's House on Chrystie Street and looking around at all the fellow workers and thinking how hopeless it was for us to try to keep up appearances. The walls are painted a warm yellow, the ceiling has been done by generous volunteers, and there are large, brightly colored icon-like paintings on wood and some colorful banners with texts (now fading out) and the great crucifix brought in by some anonymous friend with the request that we hang it in the room where the breadline eats. (Some well-meaning guest tried to improve on the black iron by gilding it, and I always intend to do something about it and restore its former grim glory.)

I looked around and the general appearance of the place was, as usual, home-like, informal, noisy, and comfortably warm on a cold evening. And yet, looked at with the eyes of a visitor, our place must look dingy indeed, filled as it always is with men and women, some children too, all of whom bear the unmistakable mark of misery and destitution. Aren't we deceiving ourselves, I am sure many of them think, in the work we are doing? What are we accomplishing for them anyway, or for the world or for the common good? "Are these people being rehabilitated?" is the question we get almost daily from visitors or from our readers (who seem to be great letter writers). One priest had his catechism classes write us questions as to our work after they had the assignment in religion class to read my book *The Long Loneliness*. The majority of them asked the same question: "How can you see Christ in people?" And we only say: It is an act of faith, constantly repeated. It is an act of love, resulting from an act of faith. It is an act of hope, that we can awaken these same acts in their hearts, too, with the help of God, and the Works of Mercy, which you, our readers, help us to do, day in and day out over the years.

On Easter Day, on awakening late after the long midnight services in our parish church, I read over the last chapter of the four Gospels and felt that I received great light and understanding with the reading of them. "They have taken the Lord out of His tomb and we do not know where they have laid Him," Mary Magdalene said, and we can say this with her in times of doubt and questioning. How do we know we believe? How do we know we indeed have faith? Because we have seen His hands and His feet in the poor around us. He has shown Himself to us in them. We start by loving them for Him, and we soon love them for themselves, each one a unique person, most special!

In that last glorious chapter of St. Luke, Jesus told His followers, "Why are you so perturbed? Why do questions arise in your minds? Look at My hands and My feet. It is I Myself. Touch Me and see. No ghost has flesh and bones as you can see I have." They were still unconvinced, for it seemed too good to be true. "So He asked them, 'Have you anything to eat?' They offered Him a piece of fish they had cooked which He took and ate before their eyes."

How can I help but think of these things every time I sit down at Chrystie Street or Peter Maurin Farm and look around at the tables filled with the unutterably poor who are going through their long-continuing crucifixion. It is most surely an exercise of faith for us to see Christ in each other. But it is through such exercise that we grow and the joy of our vocation assures us we are on the right path.

Most certainly, it is easier to believe now that the sun warms us, and we know that buds will appear on the sycamore trees in the wasteland across from the Catholic Worker office, that life will spring out of the dull clods of that littered park across the way. There are wars and rumors of war, poverty and plague, hunger and pain. Still, the sap is rising, again there is the resurrection of spring, God's continuing promise to us that He is with us always, with His comfort and joy, if we will only ask.

The mystery of the poor is this: That they are Jesus, and what you do for them you do for Him. It is the only way we have of knowing and believing in our love. The mystery of poverty is that by sharing in it, making ourselves poor in giving to others, we increase our knowledge of and belief in love.

58

Jesus' Reminders

Philip Yancey

THE IMAGE JESUS LEFT with the world, the cross, the most common image in the Christian religion, is proof that God cares about our suffering and pain. He died of it. Today the image is coated with gold and worn around the necks of beautiful girls, a symbol of how far we can stray from the reality of history. But it stands, unique among all religions of the world. Many of them have gods. But only one has a God who cared enough to become a man and to die.

Dorothy Sayers says:

For whatever reason God chose to make man as he is—limited and suffering and subject to sorrows and death—he had the honesty and courage to take his own medicine. Whatever game he is playing with his creation, he has kept his own rules and played fair. He can exact nothing from man that he has not exacted from himself. He has himself gone through the whole human experience, from the trivial irritations of family life and the cramping restrictions of hard work and lack of money to the worst horrors of pain and humiliation, defeat, despair, and death. When he was a man, he played the man. He was born in poverty and died in disgrace and thought it well worthwhile.

To some, the image of a pale body glimmering on a dark night whispers of defeat. What good is a God who does not control his Son's suffering? What possible good could such a God do for us? But a louder sound can be heard: the shout of a God crying out to man, "I *love you*." Love was compressed for all history in that lonely, bleeding figure. Jesus, who said he could call down the angels at any moment and rescue himself from the horror, chose not to–because of us. For God so loved us, that he sent his only Son to die for us.

What practical effect does Christ's identification have on the person who actually suffers? A dramatic example of the effect of this truth was seen in the ministry of Dr. Paul Brand while he was working among leprosy patients in Vellore, India. There he preached a sermon, one of his best known and best loved. At the time, Brand and his workers were among the few in the area who would touch or closely approach a person with Hansen's disease – townspeople quarantined them. Brand slipped in late to a patients' gathering, sitting on the mat at the edge of an open courtyard. The air was heavy with combined odors of crowding bodies, poverty, stale spices, treated bandages.

The patients insisted on a few words from Dr. Brand, and he reluctantly agreed. He stood for a moment, empty of ideas, looking at the patients before him. His eyes were drawn to their hands, dozens of them, most pulled inward in the familiar "leprosy claw-hand," some with no fingers, some with a few stumps. Many patients sat on their hands or otherwise hid them from view.

"I am a hand surgeon," he began, and waited for the translation into Tamil and Hindi. "So when I meet people, I can't help looking at their hands. The palmist claims he can tell your future by looking at your hands. I can tell your past. For instance, I can tell what your trade has been by the position of the calluses and the condition of the nails. I can tell a lot about your character; I love hands."

He paused and looked at the eager faces. "How I would love to have had the chance to meet Christ and study his hands! But knowing what he was like, I can almost picture them, feel them."

He paused again, then wondered aloud what it would have been like to meet Christ and study his hands. He traced the hands of Christ, beginning with infancy when his hands were small, helpless, futilely grasping. Then came the hands of the boy Jesus, clumsily holding a brush or stylus, trying to form letters of the alphabet. Then the hands of Christ the carpenter – rough, gnarled, with broken fingernails and bruises from working with saw and hammer.

Then there were the hands of Christ the physician, the healer. Compassion and sensitivity seemed to radiate from them, so much so that when he touched people they could feel something of the divine spirit coming through. Christ touched the blind, the diseased, the needy.

"Then," continued Dr. Brand, "there were his crucified hands. It hurts me to think of a nail being driven through the center of my hand, because I know what goes on there, the tremendous complex of tendons and nerves and blood vessels and muscles. It's impossible to drive a spike through its center without crippling it. The thought of those healing hands being crippled reminds me of what Christ was prepared to endure. In that act he identified himself with all the deformed and crippled human beings in the world. Not only was he able to endure poverty with the poor, weariness with the tired, but—clawed hands with the cripple."

The effect on the listening patients, all social outcasts, was electrifying. Jesus—a cripple, with a claw-hand like theirs?

Brand continued. "And then there were his resurrected hands. One of the things I find most astounding is that, though we think of the future life as something perfected, when Christ appeared to his disciples he said, 'Come look at my hands,' and he invited Thomas to put his finger into the print of the nail. Why did he want to keep the wounds of his humanity? Wasn't it because he wanted to carry back with him an eternal reminder of the sufferings of those on earth? He carried the marks of suffering so he could continue to understand the needs of those suffering. He wanted to be forever one with us."

As he finished, Paul Brand was again conscious of hands as they were lifted, all over the courtyard, palm to palm in the Indian gesture of respect, *namaste*. The hands were the same stumps, the same missing fingers and crooked arches. Yet no one tried to hide them. They were held high, close to the face, in respect for Brand, but also with new pride and dignity. God's own response to suffering made theirs easier.

T. S. Eliot wrote in one of his *Four Quartets*:

> The wounded surgeon plies the steel
> That questions the distempered part;
> Beneath the bleeding hands we feel
> The sharp compassion of the healer's art
> Resolving the enigma of the fever chart.

The surgery of life hurts. It helps me, though, to know that the Surgeon himself, the Wounded Surgeon, has felt every stab of pain and every sorrow.

New Life

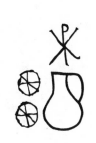

THE EVERLASTING MERCY

John Masefield

...All earthly things that blessèd morning
Were everlasting joy and warning.
The gate was Jesus' way made plain,
The mole was Satan foiled again,
Black blinded Satan snouting way
Along the red of Adam's clay;
The mist was error and damnation,
The lane the road unto salvation.
Out of the mist into the light,
O blessèd gift of inner sight.
The past was faded like a dream;
There come the jingling of a team,
A ploughman's voice, a clink of chain,
Slow hoofs, and harness under strain.
Up the slow slope a team came bowing,
Old Callow at his autumn ploughing,
Old Callow, stooped above the hales,
Ploughing the stubble into wales.
His grave eyes looking straight ahead,
Shearing a long straight furrow red;

His plough-foot high to give it earth
To bring new food for men to birth.
O wet red swathe of earth laid bare,
O truth, O strength, O gleaming share,
O patient eyes that watch the goal,
O ploughman of the sinner's soul.
O Jesus, drive the coulter deep
To plough my living man from sleep.

…Then the chains chack, the brasses jingle,
The lean reins gather through the cringle,
The figures move against the sky,
The clay wave breaks as they go by.
I kneeled there in the muddy fallow,
I knew that Christ was there with Callow,
That Christ was standing there with me,
That Christ had taught me what to be,
That I should plough, and as I ploughed
My Savior Christ would sing aloud,
And as I drove the clods apart
Christ would be ploughing in my heart,
Through rest-harrow and bitter roots,
Through all my bad life's rotten fruits.
O Christ who holds the open gate,
O Christ who drives the furrow straight,
O Christ, the plough, O Christ, the laughter

Of holy white birds flying after,
Lo, all my heart's field red and torn,
And Thou wilt bring the young green corn,
The young green corn divinely springing,
The young green corn forever singing;
And when the field is fresh and fair
Thy blessèd feet shall glitter there,
And we will walk the weeded field,
And tell the golden harvest's yield,
The corn that makes the holy bread
By which the soul of man is fed,
The holy bread, the food unpriced,
Thy everlasting mercy, Christ...

John Masefield · 329

59

I, Like the Thief

Leo Tolstoy

FIVE YEARS AGO I came to believe in Christ's teachings, and my life suddenly changed; I ceased to desire
what I had previously desired, and began to desire what
I formerly did not want. What had previously seemed
to me good seemed evil, and what seemed evil seemed
good. It happened to me as it happens to a man who
goes out on some business and suddenly decides that
the business is unnecessary and returns home. All that
was on his right is now on his left, and all that was on
his left is now on his right; his former wish to get as far
as possible from home has changed into a wish to be
as near as possible to it. The direction of my life and
my desires became different, and good and evil changed
places...

I, like that thief on the cross, have believed Christ's teaching and been saved. This is no far-fetched comparison, but the closest expression of the condition of spiritual despair and horror at the problem of life and death in which I lived formerly, and of the condition of peace and happiness in which I am now. I, like the thief, knew that I had lived and was living badly. I, like the thief, knew that I was unhappy and suffering. I, like the thief to the cross, was nailed by some force to a life of suffering and evil. And as, after the meaningless sufferings and evils of life, the thief awaited the terrible darkness of death, so did I await the same thing.

In all this I was exactly like the thief, but the difference was that the thief was already dying, while I was still living. The thief might believe that his salvation lay there beyond the grave, but I could not be satisfied with that, because besides a life beyond the grave, life still awaited me here. And I did not understand that life. It seemed to me terrible. But suddenly I heard the words of Christ and understood them, and life and death ceased to seem evil, and instead of despair I experienced happiness and the joy of life undisturbed by death.

60

Redemption

Fyodor Dostoevsky

The speaker is Dostoevsky's character Father Zossima, who, hours before his death, relates to his fellow monks the story of his conversion, in which his only brother, Markel, played a crucial role.

BELOVED FATHERS AND TEACHERS, I was born in a remote northern province, in the town of V—, of a noble father, but not of the high nobility, and not of very high rank. He died when I was only two years old, and I do not remember him at all. He left my mother a small wooden house and some capital, not a big sum, but enough to keep her and her children without want. And mother had only the two of us: myself, Zinovy, and my older brother, Markel. He was about eight years older than I, hot-tempered and irritable by nature, but kind, not given to mockery, and strangely silent, especially at home with me, mother, and the servants. He was a good student, but did not make friends with his schoolmates, though he did not quarrel with them either, at least not that our mother remembered. Half a year before his death, when he was already past seventeen, he took to visiting a certain solitary man of our town, a political exile it seems, exiled to our town from Moscow for freethinking. This exile was a great scholar and distinguished philosopher at the university. For some reason he came to love Markel and welcomed his visits. The young man spent whole evenings with him, and did so through the whole winter, until the exile was called back to government service in Petersburg, at his own request, for he had his protectors.

The Great Lent came, but Markel did not want to fast, swore and laughed at it: "It's all nonsense, there isn't any God," so that he horrified mother and the servants, and me, too, his little brother, for though I was only nine years old, when I heard those words I was very much afraid. Our servants were all serfs, four of them, all bought in the name of a landowner we knew. I also remember how mother sold one of the four, the cook Anfimia, who was lame and elderly, for sixty paper roubles, and hired a free woman in her place.

And so, in the sixth week of Lent, my brother suddenly grew worse – he had always been unhealthy, with bad lungs, of weak constitution and inclined to consumption; he was tall, but thin and sickly, yet of quite pleasing countenance. Perhaps he had caught a cold or something, in any case the doctor came and soon whispered to mother that his consumption was of the galloping sort, and that he would not live through spring. Mother started weeping; she started asking my brother cautiously (more so as not to alarm him) to observe Lent and take communion of the divine and holy mysteries, because he was then still on his feet. Hearing that, he became angry and swore at God's Church, but still he grew thoughtful: he understood at once that he was dangerously ill, and that that was why his mother was urging him, while he was still strong enough, to go to church and receive communion. He knew himself that he had been sick for a long time; already a year before he had once said coolly at the table, to mother and me: "I'm not long for this world among you, I may not live another year," and now it was as if he had foretold it.

About three days went by, and then came Holy Week. And on Tuesday morning my brother started keeping the fast and going to church. "I'm doing it only for your sake, mother, to give you joy and peace," he said to her. Mother wept from joy, and also from grief: "His end must be near, if there is suddenly such a change in him." But he did not go to church for long, he took to his bed, so that he had to confess and receive communion at home.

The days grew bright, clear, fragrant—Easter was late that year. All night, I remember, he used to cough, slept badly, but in the morning he would always get dressed and try to sit in an armchair. So I remember him: he sits, quiet and meek, he smiles, he is sick but his countenance is glad, joyful.

He was utterly changed in spirit—such a wondrous change had suddenly begun in him! Our old nanny would come into his room: "Dear, let me light the lamp in front of your icon." And before, he would never let her, he even used to blow it out.

"Light it, my dear, light it, what a monster I was to forbid you before! You pray to God as you light the icon lamp, and I pray, rejoicing at you. So we are praying to the same God."

These words seemed strange to us, and mother used to go to her room and weep, but when she went to him she wiped her eyes and put on a cheerful face. "Mother, don't weep, my dear," he would say, "I still have a long time to live, a long time to rejoice with you, and life, life is gladsome, joyful!"

"Ah, my dear, what sort of gladness is there for you, if you burn with fever all night and cough as if your lungs were about to burst?"

"Mama," he answered her, "do not weep, life is paradise, and we are all in paradise, but we do not want to know it, and if we did want to know it, tomorrow there would be paradise the world over." And everyone marveled at his words, he spoke so strangely and so decisively; everyone was moved and wept.

Acquaintances came to visit us: "My beloved," he would say, "my dear ones, how have I deserved your love, why do you love such a one as I, and how is it that I did not know it, that I did not appreciate it before?" When the servants came in, he told them time and again: "My beloved, my dear ones, why do you serve me, am I worthy of being served? If God were to have mercy on me and let me live, I would begin serving you, for we must all serve each other."

Mother listened and shook her head: "My dear, it's your illness that makes you talk like that."

"Mama, my joy," he said, "it is not possible for there to be no masters and servants, but let me also be the servant of my servants, the same as they are to me. And I shall also tell you, dear mother, that each of us is guilty in everything before everyone, and I most of all."

At that mother even smiled, she wept and smiled: "How can it be," she said, "that you are the most guilty before everyone? There are murderers and robbers, and how have you managed to sin so that you should accuse yourself most of all?"

"Dear mother, heart of my heart," he said (he had then begun saying such unexpected, endearing words), "heart of my heart, my joyful one, you must know that verily each of us is guilty before everyone, for everyone and everything. I do not know how to explain it to you, but I feel it so strongly that it pains me. And how could we have lived before, getting angry, and not knowing anything?"

Thus he awoke every day with more and more tenderness, rejoicing and all atremble with love. The doctor used to come to us: "Well, what do you think, doctor, shall I live one more day in the world?" he would joke with him.

"Not just one day, you will live many days," the doctor would answer. "You will live months and years, too."

"But what are years, what are months!" he would exclaim. "Why count the days, when even one day is enough for a man to know all happiness. My dears, why do we quarrel, boast before each other, remember each other's offenses? Let us go to the garden, let us walk and play and love and praise and kiss each other, and bless our life."

"He's not long for this world, your son," the doctor said to mother as she saw him to the porch. "From sickness he is falling into madness."

The windows of his room looked onto the garden, and our garden was very shady, with old trees; the spring buds were already swelling on the branches, the early birds arrived, chattering, singing through his windows. And suddenly, looking at them and admiring them, he began to ask their forgiveness, too: "Birds of God, joyful birds, you, too, must forgive me, because I have also sinned before you." None of us could understand it then, but he was weeping with joy: "Yes," he said, "there was so much of God's glory around me: birds, trees, meadows, sky, and I alone lived in shame, I alone dishonored everything, and did not notice the beauty and glory of it at all."

"You take too many sins upon yourself," mother used to weep.

"Dear mother, my joy, I am weeping from gladness, not from grief; I want to be guilty before them, only I cannot explain it to you, for I do not even know how to love them. Let me be sinful before everyone, but so that everyone will forgive me, and that is paradise. Am I not in paradise now?"

And there was much more that I cannot recall or set down. I remember once I came into his room alone, when no one was with him. It was a bright evening, the sun was setting and lit up the whole room with its slanting rays. He beckoned when he saw me. I went over to him; he took me by the shoulders with both hands, looked tenderly, lovingly into my face; he did not say anything, he simply looked at me like that for about a minute: "Well," he said, "go now, play, live for me!" I walked out then and went to play.

And later in life I remembered many times, with tears now, how he told me to live for him. He spoke many more such wondrous and beautiful words, though we could not understand them then. He died in the third week after Easter, conscious, and though he had already stopped speaking, he did not change to his very last hour: he looked joyfully, with gladness in his eyes, seeking us with his eyes, smiling to us, calling us. There was much talk even in town about his end. It all shook me then, but not deeply, though I cried very much when he was being buried. I was young, a child, but it all remained indelibly in my heart, the feeling was hidden there. It all had to rise up and respond in due time. And so it did.

61

I Had Been Waiting

Alfred Kazin

But when that which is perfect is come, then that which is in part shall be done away. When I was a child, I spake as a child, I understood as a child, I thought as a child; but when I became a man, I put away childish things. For now we see through a glass, darkly; but then face to face: now I know in part; but then shall I know even as also I am known.

I CORINTHIANS 13:10–12

THE MAN FROM WHOM I had accepted the little blue volume on the Fifth Avenue steps of the Library had said to me in Yiddish, searching my face doubtfully: "You *are* a Jew? You will really look into it?" No, I was not really looking into it; I could not read more than two or three pages at a time without turning away in excitement and shame. Would the old women across the street ever have believed it? But how square and hardy the words looked in their even black type. Each seemed to burn separately in the sun as I nervously flipped the pages and then turned back to where the book most naturally lay flat: *For now we see through a glass, darkly.* Each time my eye fell on that square, even, black type, the sentence began to move in the sun. It rose up, a smoking frame of dark glass above the highest roofs, steadily and joyfully burning, as, reading aloud to myself, I tasted the rightness of each word on my tongue.

It was like heaping my own arms with gifts. There were images I did not understand, but which fell on my mind with such slow opening grandeur that once I distinctly heard the clean and fundamental cracking of trees. First the image, then the thing; first the word in its taste and smell and touch, then the thing it meant, when you were calm enough to look. Images were instantaneous; the meaning alone could be like the unyielding metal taste when you bit on an empty spoon. The initial shock of that language left no room in my head for anything else. But now, each day I turned back to that little blue testament, I had that same sense of instant connectedness...

First the image, then the sense. First those clouds moving blue and white across the nearest roofs; and then the journey into that other land of summer, eternal summer, through which he had walked, wrapped in a blue and white prayer shawl, and looking back at me with the heartbreaking smile of recognition from a fellow Jew, had said: *The blind receive their sight, and the lame walk, the lepers are cleansed, and the deaf hear, the dead are raised up, and the poor have the gospel preached to them.*

And blessed is he, whosoever shall not be offended in me.

Offended in him? I had known him instantly. Surely I had been waiting for him all my life—our own Yeshua, misunderstood by his own, like me, but the very embodiment of everything I had waited so long to hear from a Jew—a great contempt for the minute daily business of the world; a deep and joyful turning back into our own spirit. It was *he*, I thought, who would resolve for me at last the ambiguity and the long ache of being a Jew—Yeshua, our own long-lost Jesus, speaking straight to the mind and heart at once. For that voice, that exultantly fiery

Alfred Kazin · 343

and tender voice, there were no gaps between images and things, for constantly walking before the Lord, he remained all energy and mind, thrust his soul into every corner of the world, and passing gaily under every yoke, remained free to seek our God in His expected place.

How long I had been waiting for him, how long: like metal for a magnet to raise it. I had recognized him immediately, and all over: that exaltation; those thorny images that cut you with their overriding fervor and gave you the husk of every word along with the kernel; that furious old Jewish impatience with *Success,* with comfort, with eating, with the rich, with the whole shabby superficial fashionable world itself; that fatigue, as of a man having constantly to make his way up and down the world on foot; and then that sternness and love that gushed out of him when he turned to the others and said: *For verily I say unto you, Till heaven and earth pass, one jot or one tittle shall in no wise pass from the law, till all be fulfilled.*

Yeshua my Yeshua! What had he to do with those who killed his own and worshiped him as God? Why would they call him only by that smooth Greek name of Jesus? He was Yeshua, my own Reb Yeshua, of whose terrible death I could never read without bursting into tears—Yeshua, our own Yeshua, the most natural of us all, the most direct, the most enchanted, and as he sprang up from the heart of poor Jews, all the dearer to me because he could now return to his own kind: *and the poor have the gospel preached to them.*

62

The Christ of Experience

E. Stanley Jones

The death of Jesus is for us nothing if we have not died with him; the resurrection of our Lord is for us nothing if we have not been raised with him.　　　　　**EMIL BRUNNER**

THE EARLY DISCIPLES had little ritual but a mighty realization. They went out not remembering Christ, but experiencing him. He was not a mere fair and beautiful story to remember with gratitude – he was a living, redemptive, actual presence then and there. They went out with the joyous and grateful cry, "Christ lives in me!" The Jesus of history had become the Christ of experience.

Some have suggested that the early Christians conquered the pagan world because they out-thought, outlived and out-died the pagans. But that was not enough: they out-experienced them. Without that they would have lacked the vital glow.

If, as it has been suggested, all great literature is autobiography, then all great appeals to the non-Christian world must be a witness. When I was called to the ministry I had a vague notion that I was to be God's lawyer—I was to argue his case for him. When I told my pastor of my call he surprised me by asking me to preach my first sermon on a certain Sunday night. I prepared very thoroughly, for I was anxious to make a good impression and argue God's case acceptably. There was a large crowd there full of expectancy, wishing me well.

I began on rather a high key. I had not gone a half dozen sentences when I used a word I had never used before (nor have I used it since!)—"indifferentism." I saw a college girl in the audience put down her head and smile. It so upset me that when I came back to the thread of my discourse, it was gone—absolutely. I do not know how long I stood there rubbing my hands, hoping that something would come back. It seemed like forever. Finally I blurted out, "Friends, I am very sorry, but I have forgotten my sermon!"

I started down the steps leading from the pulpit in shame and confusion. This was the beginning of my ministry, I thought–a total failure. As I was about to leave the pulpit a Voice seemed to say to me, "Haven't I done anything for you?"

"Yes," I replied, "You have done everything for me."

"Well," said the Voice, "couldn't you tell them that?"

"Yes, I suppose I could," I eagerly replied. So instead of going to my seat I came around in front of the pulpit below (I felt very lowly by this time and was persuaded I did not belong up there!) and said: "Friends, I see I cannot preach, but I love Jesus. You know what my life was in this community–that of a wild, reckless young man–and you know what it now is. You know he has made life new for me, and though I cannot preach I am determined to love and serve him."

At the close a lad came up and said, "Stanley, I wish I could find what you have found." He did find it then and there. The Lord let me down with a terrible thump, but I got the lesson never to be forgotten: In my ministry I was to be, not God's lawyer, but his witness.

We cannot merely talk about Christ–we must bring him. He must be a living vital reality–closer than breathing and nearer than hands and feet. We must be "God-bearers."

A Hindu lawyer recognized this and said to me one day, "What you Christians and the church need today is a new Pentecost." I knew what he meant—we need our faith to be a well of water within us springing up into everlasting life.

A friend of mine went into a shoe shop and found the shopkeeper, a Hindu, in deep distress. He had lost his only son. To comfort him, my friend said, "Well, my brother, remember in your trouble that God is love." The man's face brightened up and he said, "Yes, I know God is love."

My friend, interested at this evident eagerness, asked, "How do you know God is love?"

"Oh," said the Hindu, "I worked for Foy sahib in Cawnpore, and no one could work for Foy sahib and not know God is love."

Here was a witness with the whole of life behind it. Forty years of beautiful living was speaking to this Hindu man in his hour of distress. The Christ of experience, backed by exemplary living, is almost irresistible.

63

Christ Rising

Christoph Friedrich Blumhardt

The crowning evidence that Jesus was alive was not a vacant grave, but a spirit-filled fellowship. Not a rolled-away stone, but a carried-away church. **CLARENCE JORDAN**

IT IS NOT ENOUGH to celebrate Easter and say "Christ is risen." It is useless to proclaim this unless at the same time we can say that *we* have also risen, that we have received something from heaven. We must feel appalled when the tremendous events that took place, the death and resurrection of Jesus, are proclaimed again and again and yet actually nothing happens with us. It has no effect.

The long passage of time has brought with it a temptation to keep on speaking about the death of Christ and his resurrection without being moved by it. We hear about Christ's death on the cross, and we sit there just as bored as if we were reading a newspaper—in fact we would find a newspaper a good deal more interesting.

Though people get into tremendous arguments about religious questions, all the time God is dead. And it is perfectly all right with them if he is dead, because then they can do what they like. Nietzsche said, "God is dead," and he is right. But we say, "God is alive!" We don't want a good life, either in this one or in the next. All we want is to know that God is alive. I don't want a minute of easy happiness until this earth knows that God is alive!

We must bow down before the living God and weep aloud for having killed him up to now. We are born for trouble, born for battle. Shame on us Christians who always want to have it nice and soft, with only a bit of God in our lives!

Christ's future is not one single point in an absolute remoteness for which we are to wait, a mere coming event. This is hardly thinkable, for we would probably all go to sleep over it. Christ's future is now, or it is not at all.

We must become filled with zeal, with joy and gratitude, gladly enduring anything, however hard, in order to be free of death and of this life in the midst of death. Then the powers of the resurrection come closer to us; then Christ really becomes the risen one, and a new life comes into being. Not the kind of life we have been seeking until now, trying to be a little better than other people, thinking that it is a new life if we steal a little less or walk around a little more decently than before or wear a more respectable coat, or if we exchange a criminal's cap for something more acceptable. All this is supposed to be a new life? Bah!

It is not at all a question of being better than you were before. The new life means that forces for life can now be seen within you, that something of God and of heaven, something holy, can grow in you. It means we can actually see that it is no longer the sinful desires that have power, but Christ's resurrection, and his life, which leads you toward wholeness.

What is God's kingdom anyway? Certainly not Christian causes or institutions. God's kingdom is the power of God. It is the rulership of God. God's kingdom is the revelation of the divine life here on earth, the birth of new hearts, new minds, new feelings, new possibilities. This is God's kingdom.

Jesus has come from God to triumph over death. Jesus Christ has come into our midst as one of us so that death can be conquered. He has laid the foundation for a completely new life, a new order. In him we can become completely different men and women in the very depth of our beings.

What stupid people Christians often are! Most Christians have absolutely nothing worth saying simply because they have so little to show. The new life that Christ came to bring never quite reaches into the temporal and earthly things, never overcomes this world.

We must make a completely new beginning. I keep coming back to this same point. We need to begin completely anew again and again, more deeply, more thoroughly, more fully. We must do this until we really have laid a new foundation for the Savior. For if we really reach a point where we are united with Christ in a death like his, we shall certainly be united with him in a resurrection like his. Then we will enter into a completely new life. What a tremendous thing it is to meet the resurrection!

Christoph Friedrich Blumhardt · 353

The resurrection does not consist solely of what happened in the past, nor of what we happen to believe about it—those are not the essential things. We do not gain much by just accepting that Christ died and rose again. People may say they believe this, and still be on their way to hell. This belief is of no help unless you and I experience Jesus as Lord.

It is not the worst if some people are unable to believe that Christ rose from the dead—at least they still regard it as something tremendous, too tremendous to glibly confess. The sad thing is that so many people today claim to believe it, and yet it means so little to them. It has no effect in their lives. But there is resurrection today just as much as there was back then, after Christ's death. There is resurrection—for with a certain part of our inner being we can be in a completely different place, where most people don't dare to go. Our renewal is real to the extent that we find ourselves in an entirely different order.

Again and again Christ arises anew. In what we know of the risen Christ, God wants to renew all things. His will is for the earth as much as it is for the heavens. Otherwise we would never know his reality. We could never conceive of anything becoming different. We would think that his resurrected life was some spiritual thing that we human beings could not understand. That is not the case. No. The power of his resurrection is something within our reach.

New possibilities can dawn on us, and the more we sense these new possibilities, either in our bodies or in our souls, the more we can ask for, the more we can look for higher and greater things here on earth. Actually, there are no limits. And for this reason we can bring hope into everything, into our daily life, into everything at which we work and into anything that we touch. The power that comes from God is ready to be brought into our human situation, and in such a way as to transform it.

Therefore, we must not turn our attention to the darkness, the evils, and the imperfections of the earth, nor are we to try to figure out how this or that matter is going to turn out. All that has nothing to do with us. We are simply to ask Jesus to give us more and more of his resurrection, until it runs over, until the extraordinary powers from on high that are within our reach can get down to work on all that we do.

Christoph Friedrich Blumhardt · 355

64

Calvary Love

Amy Carmichael

IF I BELITTLE THOSE whom I am called to serve, talk of their weak points in contrast perhaps with what I think of as my strong points; if I adopt a superior attitude, forgetting "Who made thee to differ? And what hast thou that thou hast not received?" then I know nothing of Calvary love.

If I find myself half-carelessly taking lapses for granted, "Oh, that's what they always do," "Oh, of course she talks like that, he acts like that," then I know nothing of Calvary love.

If I can enjoy a joke at the expense of another; if I can in any way slight another in conversation, or even in thought, then I know nothing of Calvary love.

If I can write an unkind letter, speak an unkind word, think an unkind thought without grief and shame, then I know nothing of Calvary love.

If I do not feel far more for the grieved Savior than for my worried self when troublesome things occur, then I know nothing of Calvary love.

If I can rebuke without a pang, then I know nothing of Calvary love.

If my attitude be one of fear, not faith, about one who has disappointed me; if I say, "Just what I expected" if a fall occurs, then I know nothing of Calvary love.

If I am afraid to speak the truth, lest I lose affection, or lest the one concerned should say, "You do not understand," or because I fear to lose my reputation for kindness; if I put my own good name before the other's highest good, then I know nothing of Calvary love.

If I am content to heal a hurt slightly, saying "Peace, peace," where there is no peace; if I forget the poignant word "Let love be without dissimulation" and blunt the edge of truth, speaking not right things but smooth things, then I know nothing of Calvary love.

If I hold on to choices of any kind, just because they are my choice, then I know nothing of Calvary love.

Amy Carmichael · 357

If I am soft to myself and slide comfortably into self-pity and self-sympathy; if I do not by the grace of God practice fortitude, then I know nothing of Calvary love.

If I myself dominate myself, if my thoughts revolve round myself, if I am so occupied with myself I rarely have "a heart at leisure from itself," then I know nothing of Calvary love.

If, the moment I am conscious of the shadow of self crossing my threshold, I do not shut the door, and keep that door shut, then I know nothing of Calvary love.

If I cannot in honest happiness take the second place (or the twentieth); if I cannot take the first without making a fuss about my unworthiness, then I know nothing of Calvary love.

If I take offense easily, if I am content to continue in a cool unfriendliness, though friendship be possible, then I know nothing of Calvary love.

If I feel injured when another lays to my charge things that I know not, forgetting that my sinless Savior trod this path to the end, then I know nothing of Calvary love.

If I feel bitter toward those who condemn me, as it seems to me, unjustly, forgetting that if they knew me as I know myself they would condemn me much more, then I know nothing of Calvary love.

If souls can suffer alongside, and I hardly know it, because the spirit of discernment is not in me, then I know nothing of Calvary love.

If the praise of others elates me and their blame depresses me; if I cannot rest under misunderstanding without defending myself; if I love to be loved more than to love, to be served more than to serve, then I know nothing of Calvary love.

If I crave hungrily to be used to show the way of liberty to a soul in bondage, instead of caring only that it be delivered; if I nurse my disappointment when I fail, instead of asking that to another the word of release may be given, then I know nothing of Calvary love.

If I do not forget about such a trifle as personal success, so that it never crosses my mind, or if it does, is never given room there; if the cup of flattery tastes sweet to me, then I know nothing of Calvary love.

If in the fellowship of service I seek to attach a friend to myself, so that others are caused to feel unwanted; if my friendships do not draw others deeper in, but are ungenerous (to myself, for myself), then I know nothing of Calvary love.

Amy Carmichael · 359

If I refuse to allow one who is dear to me to suffer for the sake of Christ, if I do not see such suffering as the greatest honor that can be offered to any follower of the Crucified, then I know nothing of Calvary love.

If I slip into the place that can be filled by Christ alone, making myself the first necessity to a soul instead of leading it to fasten upon Him, then I know nothing of Calvary love.

If my interest in the work of others is cool; if I think in terms of my own special work; if the burdens of others are not my burdens too, and their joys mine, then I know nothing of Calvary love.

If I wonder why something trying is allowed, and press for prayer that it may be removed; if I cannot be trusted with any disappointment, and cannot go on in peace under any mystery, then I know nothing of Calvary love.

If the ultimate, the hardest, cannot be asked of me; if my fellows hesitate to ask it and turn to someone else, then I know nothing of Calvary love.

If I covet any place on earth but the dust at the foot of the Cross, then I know nothing of Calvary love.

That which I know not, teach Thou me, O Lord, my God.

65

The Power of Forgiveness

Johann Christoph Arnold

EASTER IS FAR MORE than a holiday or a celebration; it is power. Jesus taught us to love our enemies and to bless those who persecute us. These are not just words. As his compassionate plea from the cross shows – "Father, forgive them, for they know not what they do" – he practiced what he preached. So did Stephen, the first Christian martyr, who prayed much the same thing as he was being stoned to death: "Father, do not hold this against them."

Many people, including Bible-believing Christians, dismiss such an attitude as self-destructive foolishness. How can we embrace someone intent on harming or killing us? Why not fight back in self-defense? What about justice?

All the while we eagerly pray, "Forgive us our debts, as we forgive our debtors." Familiar as they are, I often wonder whether we really mean what we say when we repeat these words from the Lord's Prayer, and whether we sufficiently consider their meaning. Besides, Jesus was adamant when it came to the issue of forgiveness: "Go, and be reconciled to your brother; then come and offer your gift...If you forgive others when they sin against you, your heavenly Father will also forgive you. But if you do not forgive others their sins, your Father will not forgive your sins" (Matthew 5:24; 6:14–15).

Refusing to forgive is tantamount to re-crucifying Christ. Instead of seeing stones rolled away, we throw stones at each other. What so many people today fail to realize is that forgiveness is a door to peace and happiness. Forgiving is not ignoring wrongdoing, but overcoming the evil inside us and in our world with love. To forgive is not just a command of Christ but the key to reconciling all that is broken in our lives and relationships. In the words of Martin Luther King, Jr.:

> Returning hate for hate multiplies hate, adding deeper darkness to a night already devoid of stars. Darkness cannot drive out darkness; only light can do that. Hate cannot drive out hate; only love can do that. Hate multi-

plies hate, violence multiplies violence, and toughness multiplies toughness in a descending spiral of destruction...Love is the only force capable of transforming an enemy into a friend. We never get rid of an enemy by meeting hate with hate; we get rid of an enemy by getting rid of enmity.

I have lived long enough to learn that failure to forgive leads down a path of destruction – of bitterness, self-hate, alienation, relentless cycles of conflict, and downright misery. But forgiveness can vanquish all such pain. Why else did Jesus command us to forgive? It can heal both the forgiver and the forgiven. In fact, it could change the world if we allowed it to. But too often we stand in its way, not daring to let it flow through us unchecked. If only we would dare!

When Christians do put Christ's command into practice by forgiving, they create a ripple effect that can touch thousands of lives and even affect the course of history. Steven McDonald, a close friend of mine and a New York City police officer, stopped to question three youths in Central Park one day in 1986. He was shot and paralyzed from the neck down. Steven had been married less than a year, and his wife was two months pregnant. Steven forgave his attacker, and in so doing found peace and purpose in his life. Despite being bound to a wheelchair and a breathing machine, Steven has traveled several times to conflict-ridden Northern Ireland to speak about reconciliation. And he regularly visits high schools to speak about the power of forgiveness to resolve personal conflicts. His life is effecting changes in people in ways neither he nor anyone else would ever have imagined prior to his assault.

When we forgive we set ourselves free from the demon of bitterness. But we also set loose the power of love in the world. When Miami native Chris Carrier was ten, a former family employee abducted him, assaulted him, shot him in the head, and left him to die in the Everglades. But Chris survived. In the years that followed, he struggled daily with the insecurity of knowing that his abductor was still at large. Recognizing that staying angry would never change anything, Chris found the strength to move on. Then, some twenty years later, he received a telephone call that changed his life again. It was the police calling to notify him that an elderly man at a local nursing home, David McAllister, had confessed to being his abductor.

Chris visited him the following day. He saw how David's body was ruined by alcoholism and that, unable to see, he was now facing death with only his regrets to keep him company. At the end of their time together, David clasped Chris's hand and told him he was sorry. As he spoke, something came over Chris like a wave. As he said later: "Why should anyone have to face death without family, friends, the joy of life – without hope? I couldn't do anything but offer him my forgiveness and friendship."

And friendship indeed. In the days that followed, Chris visited David as often as he could, usually bringing along his wife and their two daughters. They spent hours talking, reading, and even praying together, and as they did, the old man's hardness gradually melted away.

If the cross and resurrection are not just historic happenings but present realities, which I believe they are, then what we celebrate at Easter is the healing power of God's forgiveness at work in our world today. God's forgiveness can transform lives on a personal level, but it can influence events on a broader scale as well.

Such was the case in the "awakening" at Möttlingen, Germany, which began on New Year's Eve 1843, when a young man known for his wild carousing and violent temper came to the door of pastor Christoph Blumhardt to confess all his sins. This began an unprecedented wave of confessions in which one remorseful villager after another came to reveal secret sins and reconcile their differences. Pierced to the heart, people from all walks of life felt compelled from within to break out of old ways. Stolen goods were returned, enemies reconciled, infidelities and crimes (including a case of infanticide) confessed, and broken marriages restored.

Jesus offered his disciples the "keys of the kingdom." We hold the key of forgiveness in our hands. And we must choose whether or not to use it. Christ wants to use our hands, wounded as they may be, to extend his forgiveness to the world. Will they be closed, or outstretched like his?

66

The Feast of Freedom

Jürgen Moltmann

> I live each day to kill death;
> I die each day to beget life,
> and in this dying unto death,
> I die a thousand times and
> am reborn another thousand
> through that love.
>
> **JULIA ESQUIVEL**

THE EASTER FAITH recognizes that the raising of the crucified Christ from the dead provides the great alternative to this world of death. This faith sees the raising of Christ as God's protest against death, and against all the people who work for death; for the Easter faith recognizes God's passion for the life of the person who is

367

threatened by death and with death. And faith participates in this process of love by getting up out of the apathy of misery and out of the cynicism of prosperity, and fighting against death's accomplices, here and now, in this life.

Weary Christians have often enough deleted this critical and liberating power from Easter. Their faith has then degenerated into the confident belief in certain facts, and a poverty-stricken hope for the next world, as if death were nothing but a fate we meet with at the end of life. But death is an evil power now, in life's very midst. It is the economic death of the person we allow to starve; the political death of the people who are oppressed; the social death of the handicapped; the noisy death that strikes through napalm bombs and torture; and the soundless death of the apathetic soul.

The resurrection faith is not proved true by means of historical evidence, or only in the next world. It is proved here and now, through the courage for revolt, the protest against deadly powers, and the self-giving of men and women for the victory of life. It is impossible to talk convincingly about Christ's resurrection without participating in the movement of the Spirit "who descends on all flesh" to quicken it. This movement of the Spirit is the divine "liberation movement," for it is the process whereby the world is recreated.

So resurrection means rebirth out of impotence and indolence to "the living hope." And today "living hope" means a passion for life, and a lived protest against death.

Christ's resurrection is the beginning of God's rebellion. That rebellion is still going on in the Spirit of hope, and will be complete when, together with death, "every rule and every authority and power" is at last abolished (1 Cor. 15:24).

The resurrection hope finds living expression in men and women when they protest against death and the slaves of death. But it lives from something different — from the superabundance of God's future. Its freedom lives in resistance against all the outward and inward denials of life. But it does not live from this protest. It lives from joy in the coming victory of life. Protest and resistance are founded on this hope. Otherwise they degenerate into mere accusation and campaigns of revenge. But the greater hope has to take living form in this protest and resistance; otherwise it turns into religious seduction.

Easter is a feast, and it is as the feast of freedom that it is celebrated. For with Easter begins the laughter of the redeemed, the dance of the liberated and the creative play of fantasy. From time immemorial Easter hymns have celebrated the victory of life by laughing at death, mocking at hell, and ridiculing the mighty ones who spread fear and terror around them.

Easter is the feast of freedom. It makes the life which it touches a *festal* life. "The risen Christ makes life a perpetual feast," said Athanasius. But can the whole of life really be a feast? Even life's dark side—death, guilt, senseless suffering? I think it can. Once we realize that the giver of this feast is the outcast, suffering, crucified Son of Man from Nazareth, then every "no" is absorbed into this profound "yes," and is swallowed up in its victory.

Easter is at one and the same time God's protest *against* death, and the feast of freedom *from* death. Anyone who fails to hold these two things together has failed to understand the resurrection of the Christ who was crucified. Resistance is the protest of those who hope, and hope is the feast of the people who resist.

67

At God's Expense

Clarence Jordan

I DON'T BELIEVE the crucifixion was the will of God.
I've been asked: How do you fit that in with the Old
Testament concept of shedding of blood for the sins of
his people? Was not this God's son shedding his blood
as a propitiation, so to speak, for the sins of the world?

Well, I believe that it was God's will that his son
should be on this earth, that he should be in a cruci-
fiable situation. I think the kind of life he lived was
inevitably a life in the shadow of crucifixion. It was a
life in such tension with the world—it was in mortal
combat with the world—that either the world had to
die or Jesus had to die. It was a fight unto death, and I
think that God's way of love here is being a sin-bearer,

of saying, "Sure, put on me your sin...let me be your scapegoat, let me be your lamb." Now this is the very important thing. For the cross is just this. It's saying to the world, "Now you have a cross, you have a sin-bearer. If you have sin, put it on."

The reason that the world is so terribly neurotic today is that it no longer has a sin-bearer. The Church doesn't want to bear the sins of the world. We don't want to be anybody's dumping ground. We don't want to have them throwing their dirty dishwater on us. And the world has no scapegoat; it has no sin-bearer. The body of Christ is unwilling to bear the sins of the world. But God was willing to bear. And so we throw on him our sins. Behold the Lamb of God, that takes away in his own body, bearing our sins in his body up to the cross. Did God put our sins on the back of his son on the cross? No. He made him available and we put our sins on his back. Now, in the sense that God made Jesus available and expendable, God was a party to the cruci-fixion. Love makes itself available, love makes itself expendable.

I had this face me just a few weeks ago. The phone rang about 1:30 at night—we're used to all kinds of crank phone calls—usually they come late at night, and begin by somebody cussing you in a drunken tone. You generally let them talk—kind of discharge their static electricity or whatever it is that's motivating them. But this voice was very deliberate:

He said, "Who's speaking?"

I said, "Clarence Jordan."

He said, "Mr. Jordan, I just wanted to let you know that within about seventeen minutes there's going to be a green pickup truck pull out of that dirt road there just below the bridge and it's going to be loaded with dynamite. We haven't blown up your place with dynamite yet. Now we're going to blow it off the face of the map. I just wanted to call you to let you know so you would have time to get the people out of the buildings."

Well, I tell you, he scared the daylights out of me. I said, "Who's calling? Who am I speaking to?"

He said, "That isn't important."

I said, "But, brother, anyone who calls me at 1:30 at night to warn me to get these people out of the building, I owe him a debt of gratitude and I'd just like to know to whom am I grateful."

He said, *"I told you that isn't important and now you've got sixteen minutes."* BANG!

I'm standing there, 1:30 at night with a dead telephone in my hand, sixteen minutes to go. What are we going to do? The world's got to have somebody they can throw their sins on—even if it's dynamite. I stood there with that telephone in my hand, and about that time my boy called out to me and he said, "Who was it, Daddy?"

I said, "He wouldn't tell me."

"What did he want?"

"He wants to blow the place up."

He said, "Oh."

I went back to the bedroom and my wife said, "What's all that?"

I said, *"Some guy said he's going to blow this place up in sixteen minutes."*

She said, "Really?" and rolled over.

Here in an hour of crisis a man's closest don't seem to understand. They thought I was joking. "Oh?" "Really?" Well, I thought, if I were to go around to the other folks, banging on their doors and saying, "We're about to be blown up in sixteen minutes," they would say "Really?" I wouldn't get anywhere. So I crawled back into bed.

I must confess the thoughts in my head were not conducive to sound slumber. I watched that clock click off those minutes. It clicked off sixteen minutes, and when it did headlights came up the road near that bridge and I thought, "Well, this is it." But we weren't going to be out there under that light, running around in our pajamas like a bunch of scared nitwits. We were going to be in our beds. And if the world wanted to have a little blowing-up party, they could have a little blowing-up party. It just could be, it'd do them good.

If this was the way God wanted to spend us, we had always said we were expendable, that it was his business as to how he wanted to expend us. If he wanted us to go up in one big flash, that was his business. In that respect the bombing would be the will of God. In that respect the crucifixion was the will of God. But it would not be God setting a match to the fuse. It is not God driving the nails. It isn't God driving the pickup truck. It's that God is making provision for the sins of the world to be discharged.

The pickup came and slowed down, and I thought he was coming in. But he didn't. We felt this taunt that they threw at Jesus' face—"Let him save himself." He couldn't. He was the one that he couldn't save. He hadn't come in the first place to save himself. He'd come to save mankind. He was the only one who couldn't save himself. He could save others, but he could not save himself. The taunt was true. For the world had to have a lightning rod to discharge its static, spiritual energy. And God made himself available in his son. And I think God needs in this world, available people who will bear the sins of the world. Now that is what the death of Jesus means to me. He did die for our sins, and as a result of our sins. God made him available, but God didn't kill him. We did.

68

Jesus Gives All

Henri Nouwen

Jesus knew that the time had come for him to leave this world and go to the Father. Having loved his own who were in the world, he now showed them the full extent of his love…So he got up from the meal, took off his outer clothing, and wrapped a towel around his waist. After that, he poured water into a basin and began to wash his disciples' feet, drying them with the towel that was wrapped around him. **JOHN 13:1–5**

THIS AFTERNOON I took the train to Paris to celebrate the Holy Thursday liturgy with the L'Arche community, "Nomaste." It was a very moving celebration. We gathered in the community room of Nomaste. There were about forty people. In his welcome, the director of the community, Toni Paoli, expressed his vision that

L'Arche should be not simply a comfortable place for people with disabilities, but a Christian community in which people serve one another in the name of Jesus. After the Gospel reading, he again proclaimed his deep love for Jesus. Then he stood up and washed the feet of four members of his community.

After the Eucharist, a rice dish, bread, and wine were brought and put on the altar. In silence, deepened by three short Gospel readings about God's love, we shared this simple food.

Sitting in the basement room in Paris surrounded by forty poor people, I was struck again by the way Jesus concluded his active life. Just before entering on the road of his passion he washed the feet of his disciples and offered them his body and blood as food and drink. These two acts belong together. They are both an expression of God's determination to show us the fullness of his love. Therefore John introduces the story of Jesus' washing of the disciples' feet with the words: "Having loved his own who were in the world, he loved them to the end" (John 13:1).

What is even more astonishing is that on both occasions Jesus commands us to do the same. After washing his disciples' feet, Jesus says, "I have given you an example so that you may copy what I have done to you" (John 13:15). After giving himself as food and drink, he says, "Do this in remembrance of me" (Luke 22:19). Jesus calls us to continue his mission of revealing the perfect love of God in this world. He calls us to total self-giving. He does not want us to keep anything for ourselves. Rather, he wants our love to be as full, as radical, and as complete as his own. He wants us to bend ourselves to the ground and touch the places in each other that most need washing. He also wants us to say to each other, "Eat of me and drink of me." By this complete mutual nurturing, he wants us to become one body and one spirit, united by the love of God.

When Toni spoke to his community about his love for Jesus, and when I saw how he washed their feet and gave them the bread and wine, it seemed as if–for the moment–I saw a glimpse of the new kingdom Jesus came to bring. Everybody in the room knew how far he or she was from being a perfect expression of God's love. But everybody was also willing to make a step in the direction to which Jesus pointed.

It was an evening in Paris I will not easily forget.

THE WORD BECAME FLESH so as to wash my tired feet. He touches me precisely where I touch the soil, where earth connects with my body that reaches out to heaven. He kneels and takes my feet in his hands and washes them. Then he looks up at me and, as his eyes and mine meet, he says: "Do you understand what I have done for you? If I, your Lord and Master, have washed your feet, you must wash your brothers' and sisters' feet" (John 13:13–14). As I walk the long, painful journey toward the cross, I must pause on the way to wash my neighbors' feet. As I kneel before my brothers and sisters, wash their feet, and look into their eyes, I discover that it is because of my brothers and sisters who walk with me that I can make the journey at all.

69

An Invitation

Joyce Hollyday

IN THE HALF-LIGHT OF DAWN, in a graveyard, it might have been tempting to believe that their eyes were playing tricks. But the body the women had come to anoint was indeed gone, and the proclamation rang out through the eeriness and emptiness of the place: "He has risen."

Mary Magdalene and the other Mary fled from the tomb "with fear and great joy," according to Matthew's account. It was a case of mixed emotions entirely appropriate to the occasion. The women were bursting to tell the news, and yet they were afraid of what had been revealed first to them.

Before they ever reached the others, they encountered their risen Lord. He greeted them and then offered them the words of reassurance they most needed to hear: "Do not be afraid."

The words are common in the biblical narrative. At the time of Jesus' birth, another time of uncommon joy and fear, Mary, Joseph, Zechariah, and the shepherds in the fields all received the words as reassurance. "Do not be afraid" was part of Jesus' invitation to Peter to be a follower, and the same words rang out over a storm when the disciples became fearful and an overly brave Peter stepped out to walk on water.

Jesus regularly reminded his followers not to fear their enemies or the uncertainties that lay ahead. He invited three trembling disciples at his Transfiguration to discard their fear, and said to the ruler Jairus at his daughter's healing, "Do not fear, only believe."

After Jesus' crucifixion, fear ran rampant among his followers. Joseph of Arimathea, owner of the tomb, asked Pilate for Jesus' body "secretly, for fear of the Jews." Nicodemus came with spices to help prepare the body for burial, but only under the safe cover of night. And the inner circle of Jesus' disciples, who had abandoned, and in Peter's case even denied, their Lord, remained hidden behind closed doors.

Even the authorities who had put him to death were fearful. Great care was taken to securely seal the tomb. And when the news reached the chief priests that Jesus had risen, they devised a cover-up, offering money to the tomb guards to spread the story that Jesus' disciples had come and stolen the body.

Against this fear and fraud was the simple faithfulness of the women, who had stood at the cross, watched as the stone was rolled over the tomb, and come at dawn to anoint the body. Their reward was the gift of being witnesses to the Resurrection.

"Do not be afraid" were Jesus' first words to them. The message attended his birth, his ministry, his death and Resurrection. And it comes to us today with the same gentle and compelling clarity with which it was offered on that first Easter morning.

There is much around us that is awesome and awful. We know too well the divisions and suffering that plague our world. We have seen that the authorities today use tactics similar to those employed 2,000 years ago, and many people scheme to play to our fear, destroy our hope, and seal off our joy.

But we have the confidence of our faith. We have seen the risen Lord!

Mary and Mary Magdalene loved with such a perfect love that they shed their fear. Empowered by their faith and their encounter with the risen Christ, they ran on to proclaim what they had seen and what they knew to be true. As Jesus had reminded Jairus, they knew that they could not both believe and fear. They were among the first to know the truth that John later put into words: "There is no fear in love, but perfect love casts out fear" (1 John 4:18).

They challenge us to love and believe. To love Jesus with a perfect love and to believe in the power of his Resurrection. Certainly they grieved and experienced their hope flagging during the dark moments surrounding Jesus' death. But they never lost their faith. It remained a small, steady flame that was fanned to brilliant, bold new life in the light of that Easter dawn.

The women invite you and me to such faith. Their testimony stands through the ages. It is a reminder to "rekindle the gift of God that is within you...for God did not give us a spirit of timidity but a spirit of power and love" (2 Timothy 1:6–7). With courage and joy, let us claim that same spirit that dwelt within our sisters, the first witnesses of the Resurrection.

70

A New World

N. T. Wright

THE GOSPEL which Jesus preached is a direct challenge to the power structures of this world. We do not often, perhaps, think of it like that. Children of our times as we are, we like to keep politics and religion in separate and watertight compartments. But try selling that line to a Jew of the first century. Or try selling it to a Roman emperor, for whom the worship of the national gods was a vital part of what constituted obedient allegiance to himself!

Religion was woven tightly into the whole social fabric of the world, as it has been at almost all times and almost all places in human history, with only the last two centuries in certain parts of the Western world being exceptions, and even then the split is only skin deep. Result: challenge the religion, and you challenge the society. Summon people to a new allegiance to God, and you weaken their allegiance to Caesar. Or, as it may be, summon nationalist rebels to a new allegiance to God and you weaken their allegiance to the rebel cause, as they discover that their rebellion proceeded not from faith and trust but from fear and bruised arrogance. There you have, in a nutshell, the historical and political reasons why Jesus was crucified.

So when we say that the gospel of Jesus posed a threat to the established power structures, we cannot imagine that he was simply offering an alternative political solution. He wasn't coming to propose a left-wing alternative to a right-wing government, or vice versa. He was offering a new world. Up until now, the world had been shared out among the rulers of the world. Caesar and his rivals had parceled the world out between them. And the Jewish nation had been getting more and more frustrated, waiting for God to step in and give them their place in the sun. And behind Caesar and his rivals, and behind the Jewish nationalism too, we hear a more sinister claim, made by an old acquaintance in the wilderness: "To you I will give all this authority and its glory; for it has been delivered to me, and I give it to whom I will."

When people make the state a god, they make it a demon. We see it all around us in our world, too, even though a good many people would mock the idea of there being actual demons. We, too, appeal to the "forces" of economics, of political theories; or, at a personal level, to the forces of aggression and sexuality; and increasingly people talk about such forces as if they are known to be things that it is pointless to resist. The pattern is that of paganism, even though in polite society we ignore the lunatic fringe of real pagans.

When Jesus dies as a failed, bizarre, nonpolitical political Messiah, Pilate embodies for a moment the apparent triumph of Satan over Jesus. "This is your hour," says Jesus to the soldiers in the garden. "This is your hour, and the power of darkness." Satan had offered Jesus the kingdoms of the world on one condition, that he fall down and worship him. Jesus had refused to do so and the cross is the direct result of that refusal. The kingdoms of the world reject him, and kill him. And not only Rome, either. There was no room for Jesus not only in the Roman empire of his day, but also in the official Judaism of the day.

We must not imagine that when Jesus was put to death it was by second-rate religious nonsense and third-rate political ploys. It was Judaism and Rome that put Jesus on the cross: the highest religion and the finest political and governmental system that the world of that time had ever seen.

That tells us something very important about God's verdict on the whole of human affairs. But, beyond that, we can see that the whole life and ministry of Jesus has indeed been a battle with demons. Not just with the evil spirits who possessed poor lunatic souls whom Jesus set free, though they were real enough in their own way. No: the battle has been with the rulers of the world, the power structures who have organized themselves and their authority so that there is no room for God in the world. Jesus, then, has come not to offer yet one more political alternative but to break the stranglehold that the powers have on the world. He offers a new world, a world in which God is God and human beings are set free to be human beings.

And what happens to him in consequence? The rulers of this world, acting out Satan's revenge upon this one who dares to raid the strong man's house and plunder his goods, strip him naked, and hold him up to contempt in public, dancing round him and celebrating their triumph over him: "You who would destroy the temple and rebuild it in three days, save yourself!" "What I have written, I have written." But it is at precisely this point that Satan has overreached himself: because the cross is, in point of fact, not the world's victory over Jesus, but Jesus' victory over the world.

Here is the mystery, the secret, one might almost say the *cunning,* of the deep love of God: that it is bound to draw on to itself the hatred and pain and shame and anger and bitterness and rejection of the world, but to draw all those things on to itself is precisely the means, chosen from all eternity by the generous, loving God, by which to rid his world of the evils which have resulted from human abuse of God-given freedom.

Listen to what St. Paul says, taking the brutal facts of the cross and turning them inside out: "God cancelled the bond which stood against us, with its legal demands: he set it aside, nailing it to the cross." That is to say: The world, and the rulers of the world, had you in their grip. Satan had you in his power, and you could not escape. But Jesus took that bondage upon himself: it is all there in the charge which was nailed over the cross, and in Pilate's cynical use of his authority: "What I have written, I have written." Jesus took it on himself; and, being the one person who had never, in fact, submitted to the rulers of the world, the one who all along had been free of them, who had lived as a free human being, obedient to God and lovingly sovereign over the world, he beat them at their own game. *He* stripped the *rulers!* He made a public example of *them;* God, in Christ, celebrated his triumph over the prince of this world.

The cross is not a defeat, but a victory. It is the dramatic reassertion of the fact that God's love is sovereign, that the rulers of the world do not have the last word, that the kingdom of God has defeated the kingdom of Satan, that the kingdoms of the world have now become, in principle, the kingdom of our God, and of his Messiah: and he shall reign for ever and ever.

71

The Way of Peace

John Howard Yoder

He was despised and rejected by men, a man of sorrows, and familiar with suffering...He was pierced for our transgressions, he was crushed for our iniquities; the punishment that brought us peace was upon him, and by his wounds we are healed...He was assigned a grave with the wicked...though he had done no violence... **ISAIAH 53:3–9**

IN ALL AGES THESE WORDS of the prophet concerning the one he called the "Servant of the Lord" have been beloved by Christians for the portrait they paint of our crucified Master. Yet when we find these words echoing in the New Testament, it is not only because they are fitting or beautiful words to describe Christ and his sacrifice on behalf of sinful humanity; it is because they constitute a call to the Christian to do likewise. There we read:

> If you have done right and suffer for it your endurance is worthwhile in the sight of God; to this you were called, because Christ suffered on your behalf, and left you an example; it is for you to follow in his steps. (1 Pet. 2:20–21).

The innocent, silently uncomplaining suffering of Christ is not only an act of Christ on our behalf from which we benefit; it is also an example of Christ for our instruction, which we are to follow. This portrait of Christ is to be painted again on the ordinary canvas of our lives. Did not Jesus himself say that those who would follow him must deny themselves and take up their cross? What does it mean to bear a cross?

The cross of Christ was the price of his obedience to God amidst a rebellious world; it was suffering for having done right, for loving where others hated, for representing in the flesh the forgiveness and the righteousness of God among people both less forgiving and less righteous. The cross of Christ was God's method of overcoming evil with good.

The cross of the Christian is no different. It is the price of one's obedience to God's love. Such unflinching love for friend and foe alike will mean hostility and suffering for us, as it did for him.

Jesus instructed his disciples, simply and clearly, not to resist evil and to love one's enemy (Matt. 5:39–45). He was not a foolish dreamer spinning out futile hopes for a better world, thinking that if only we keep smiling everything will turn out all right, with our opponents turned into friends and our sacrifices all repaid. He knew full well the cost of such unlimited love.

"It is by this that we know what love is," says the apostle, "that Christ laid down his life for us. And we in turn are bound to lay down our lives for our brothers" (1 John 3:16).

Christians whose loyalty to the Prince of Peace puts them out of step with today's nationalistic world, because they are willing to love their nation's friends but not to hate their nation's enemies, are not unrealistic dreamers who think that by their objections they will end all wars. On the contrary, it is the soldiers who think they can put an end to wars by preparing for just one more.

John Howard Yoder · 393

Christians love their enemies because God does so, and commands his followers to do so. That is the only reason, and that is enough.

No one created in God's image and for whom Christ died can be for me an enemy, whose life I am willing to threaten or to take, unless I am more devoted to something else – to a political theory, to a nation, to the defense of certain privileges, or to my own personal welfare – than I am to God's cause: his loving invasion of this world in his prophets, his Son, and his church.

In any kind of conflict, from the fistfight to the labor dispute, from the family quarrel to the threat of international communism, the Christian sees the world and its wars from the viewpoint of the cross. "When we were God's enemies, we were reconciled to him through the death of his Son" (Rom. 5:10).

The Christian has no choice. If this was God's pattern, if his strategy for dealing with his enemies was to love them and give himself for them, it must be ours as well.

72

Spirit of Fire

Eberhard Arnold

And everyone was filled with awe, and many wonders and miraculous signs were done among the apostles. All the believers were together and had everything in common.

ACTS 2:43–44

THE BIRTH OF THE FIRST COMMUNITY of Christ in Jerusalem is too seldom taken seriously. The miraculous account of the disciples speaking in tongues is too strange for most people. The nature of the communal way of life of the early Christian church is no longer understood. And because both these decisive features of the early church are looked upon with skepticism, it is often impossible to portray this most important experience except in watered-down terms and concepts.

No one person or group could have made the first church. No heights of oratory, no flaming enthusiasm, could have awakened for Christ the thousands who were moved at the time, or produced the life-unity of the early church. The Spirit did not, as you might think, descend upon the speakers in such a way that they preached a sermon or gave a speech to an unenlightened crowd. Instead, fiery tongues of the Spirit ate their way into the hearts of the hearers and inflamed the crowd in one common experience of the same Spirit and the same Christ.

The deepest mystery of the early church lies in the very presence of the risen Christ himself, who makes his dwelling in each person's heart and reveals the power of his presence in the midst of his church. The open tomb proves that God rules because at the first Pentecost, from the one who had died and risen again, the life of the Spirit broke in as the coming of the kingdom. The crucified one had risen – that was the proclamation at Pentecost. God had wakened him from the dead and made him the Messiah and king of the coming kingdom. It was in the strength of this proclamation that the early church immersed itself.

When the murderers of Jesus stood before the spirit of the living Christ they were confronted with absolute truthfulness. Their first response surged from deep within their hearts: "What shall we do?" As a result, there came about a complete transformation of people's inner being, a reshaping of their lives, which was the very change of heart and conduct that John the Baptist had proclaimed. He had seen it as the first requirement for the great revolution to come, the turning upside down of everything. Personal rebirth could not be separated from this total transformation in Christ.

For this reason, what Jesus taught in the Sermon on the Mount was actually fulfilled in the early church, as were indeed all his words. Fellowship in his Word meant life-creating and life-shaping power. It meant the fellowship of being truly bound together in prayer and in the breaking of bread, of becoming a genuine community, embracing the whole of life. Christ came to gather his people, and thus when the Spirit descended, "All who had come to this faith remained together and had everything in common, and they sold their possessions and goods and distributed them to all, as any had need" (Acts 2:44–45). After this common experience of the Spirit, which surged up from within, there could be no question of any rules and regulations; the simple truth was that the early church was one heart and one soul.

What did the first believers experience? They experienced the kingdom of God – the revolution of all things and the revaluation of all values. They experienced the complete changing of all conditions and all possibilities, the switching of all relationships in business, state, society, and everywhere. A completely different scale of values took effect, quite different from all other values that had existed so far. God became the highest value; he reigned and revealed himself. Christ replaced the other sovereignties; he swept away the power of lying, of impurity, and of murder, and instead of them the peace of God took hold. This was the expectation and experience of the original church-community.

The Pentecost of the first church-community was nothing else than the witnessing power of the Spirit of the future, sent ahead. The church-community of Christ was nothing else than a renewed birth of Christ, a renewed incarnation of the eternal Word. This incarnation continues. It does not take place in some kind of symbolic ritual in a church service. Rather, the whole of life becomes a symbol and a ritual, so that the whole of life becomes a representation, an incarnation of the Word. The incarnation of the Spirit in church-community corresponds to the character of the final kingdom.

In Jesus' resurrected presence, the invisible kingdom of God has become visible reality. The word has taken shape, love has become real. Jesus showed what love meant. His word and life proved that love knows no bounds. Love halts at no barrier. It can never be silenced, no matter what circumstances make it seem impossible to practice it. Nothing is impossible for the faith that springs from the fire of love. For this reason, the call of Jesus does not stop at property.

When the Spirit was given by the risen one, he overturned everything and set it on fire. Then the disciples were able to become a life-sharing community, and only then did their love overflow. They were all on fire with the same burning love, which drew them irresistibly and for always together. Love had become in them a "holy must." Just as Jesus had always wanted to gather his nearest friends and pupils, whom we call disciples, so the Spirit drew the early Christians radically to one another. Together they felt compelled to live the life of

Jesus, and together, in complete community, they experienced the powers of the future.

Only in this way could isolation and its ice-cold existence be overcome. Communal life with its white-hot love began. In its heat, property was melted away to the very foundations. The icy substructures of age-old glaciers melt before God's sun. All ownership feeds on stifling self-interest. When deadly selfishness is killed by love, and only then, ownership and all that separates comes to an end. This is how it was in the early church. This is how it still can be: Under the influence of the Spirit, community is born, where people do not think in terms of "mine" and "thine."

This kind of love overlooks no need or suffering. In such a life-sharing community no one suffers a lack of clothing, food, or any other necessity of life. Those who want to keep goods and valuables for themselves in spite of the need around them must do violence to their own hearts. God's heart is never limited in its sphere of action. Those who held their goods in common at Jerusalem thus gave generous hospitality to thousands of pilgrims. Through the outpouring of the Spirit, they were able to care wisely for many, for very many, with the slenderest means.

The Pentecostal spring of the first Christian church contrasts sharply with the icy rigidity of our Christianity today. Everyone senses that at that time a fresher wind blew and purer water flowed, a stronger power and a more fiery warmth ruled than today among those of us who call ourselves Christians. We all know that in spite of the different churches, the community life of faith and love represented by the early church is almost completely absent today.

What has Christianity in general lost? What was the all-important event that took place in Jerusalem? The word of Jesus, and even more, his life and deeds from the manger to the cross, were really alive and present in that first circle of the Christ-movement. This community of faith and community of life in the first love was marked by the risen Christ—the Christ who had said, "I am with you always." Everything depends on seeing the mystery of the risen Christ as unconditional love. There is only one thing that knows no conditions: that is love. There is only one absolute: that is God's rulership. There is only one direct way: that is the experience of God's love in Jesus Christ. In Christ, his love is put into practice.

Sources and Acknowledgments

The authors below are listed in order of their appearance in this book. While every effort has been made to identify and credit copyright holders, there may still be omissions and inadvertent errors. Please contact Plough if you find one.

Jane Kenyon, "Looking at Stars," from *Collected Poems*. Copyright © 2005 by The Estate of Jane Kenyon. Reprinted with the permission of The Permissions Company, Inc. on behalf of Graywolf Press, www.graywolfpress.org.

SECTION I. INVITATION

Oscar Wilde, excerpted from "The Ballad of Reading Gaol," written in Paris, 1897; publ. 1898.

1. Kathleen Norris, "My Messy House," from *Amazing Grace*. Copyright © 1998 by Kathleen Norris. Reprinted by permission of the author and Riverhead Books, an imprint of Penguin Group (USA) LLC.

2. William Willimon, "Repent," from *On a Wild and Windy Mountain*, by William H. Willimon. Copyright © 1984 by Abingdon Press. Used by permission. All rights reserved.

3. Walter Wangerin, "In Mirrors," from *Reliving the Passion*. Copyright © 1992 by Walter Wangerin Jr. Used by permission of Zondervan, www.zondervan.com.

4. Barbara Cawthorne Crafton, "Living Lent," from *Living Lent: Meditations for These Forty Days*. Copyright © 1998 by the Church Pension Fund. All rights reserved. Used by permission of Church Publishing Incorporated, New York, NY.

5. Edna Hong, "A Look Inside," from *The Downward Ascent*. Copyright © 1979 by Augsburg Publishing House. Minneapolis, MN: Augsburg Publishing House, 1979.

6. Jean-Pierre de Caussade, "Surrender Is Everything," from *The Joy of Full Surrender*, ed. by Hal M. Helms and Robert J. Edmonston. Copyright © 2008 by Paraclete Press Inc., Brewster, MA.

7. Oswald Chambers, "The Relinquished Life," from *My Utmost for His Highest*. Copyright © 1935 by Dodd, Mead & Co., renewed 1963 by the Oswald Chambers Publication Association, Ltd. Used by permission of Discovery House Publishers, Box 3566, Grand Rapids, MI 49501. All rights reserved.

8. Thomas à Kempis, "The Royal Road," from an online edition of *The Imitation of Christ*, transl. Aloysius Croft and Harold Bolton.

9. Thomas Merton, "To Know the Cross," from *No Man Is an Island*, by Thomas Merton. Copyright © 1955 by The Abbey of Our Lady of Gethsemani and renewed 1983 by the Trustees of the Merton Legacy Trust. Reprinted by permission of Houghton Mifflin Harcourt Publishing Company. All rights reserved.

10. Dietrich Bonhoeffer, "Discipleship and the Cross," from *Meditations on the Cross*, transl. Douglas W. Stott. Louisville, KY: Westminster John Knox Press, 1998.

11. Søren Kierkegaard, "Followers, Not Admirers," from *Provocations: Spiritual Writings of Kierkegaard*, compiled and edited by Charles E. Moore (Plough, 1999).

12. J. Heinrich Arnold, "The Center," from his books *Freedom from Sinful Thoughts* (Plough, 1997) and *Discipleship* (Plough, 1994).

SECTION II. TEMPTATION

Geoffrey Hill, "Lachrimae Amantis," in *New & Collected Poems: 1952–1992*, by Geoffrey Hill. Copyright © 1994 by Geoffrey Hill. Reprinted by permission of Houghton Mifflin Harcourt Publishing Company. All rights reserved.

13. Philip Berrigan, "Keeping Watch," from "Sleeping and Watching" in *Disciples and Dissidents*. Athol, MA: Haley's, 2001. Copyright © 2001 by Steven Baggarly, Philip Berrigan, et al. Used by permission.

14. Fleming Rutledge, "The Common Criminal," from *The Undoing of Death*. Grand Rapids, MI: Wm. B. Eerdmans Publishing Co., 2002. Used by permission.

15. Emil Brunner, "The Divine Scandal," from *The Great Invitation*, transl. Harold Knight. Philadelphia, PA: Westminster Press, 1955; and from *I Believe in the Living God*, transl. & ed. John Holden. Copyright © 1961 by W. I. Jenkins. Philadelphia, PA: Westminster Press, 1961.

16. Barbara Brown Taylor, "Truth to Tell," from "The Perfect Mirror." Copyright ©1998 by Christian Century Foundation. Reprinted with permission from the March 18–25, 1998 issue of *The Christian Century*.

17. John Donne, "They Took My Lord Away," from *The Showing Forth of Christ*. New York: Harper and Row, 1964.

18. Ernesto Cardenal, "Remember Her," adapted from "The Alabaster Bottle" (Matt. 26:6-13) from *The Gospel in Solentiname*, by Ernesto Cardenal. Maryknoll, NY: Orbis Books, 1982, 2010. Used by permission.

19. Meister Eckhart, "Merchandising Truth," from *Meister Eckhart: A Modern Translation*, by Raymond Bernard Blakney. Copyright © 1941 by Harper & Brothers, renewed 1968 by Raymond Bernard Blakney. Reprinted by permission of HarperCollins Publishers.

20. John Dear, "Sheath Your Sword," from *Jesus the Rebel*. Copyright © 2000 by John Dear. Reprinted by permission of Sheed and Ward, an Apostolate of the Priests of the Sacred Heart, 7373 S. Lovers Lane Rd., Franklin WI 53132; permission conveyed through Copyright Clearance Center, Inc.

21. Romano Guardini, "Believing Is Seeing," from *Jesus Christus: Meditations*. Chicago: Henry Regnery Company, 1959.

22. Henry Drummond, "Turning," from *The Ideal Life*. London: Hodder and Stoughton, 1897.

23. Kahlil Gibran, "The Crucified," from *The Treasured Writings of Kahlil Gibran*. Edison, NJ: Castle Books, 1975.

SECTION III. PASSION

Christina Rossetti, "Beneath Thy Cross," from *Poems: Feasts and Fasts*. London: Fount Paperbacks, an imprint of HarperCollins Publishers, 1996.

24. Blaise Pascal, "The Mystery of Jesus," from *Pensées*, transl. A. J. Krailsheimer. New York: Penguin Putnam, 1995. Copyright © 1966, 1995 by A. J. Krailsheimer. Reproduced by permission of Penguin Books Ltd.

25. Jürgen Moltmann, "Prisoner of Hope," from *The Power of the Powerless*, by Jürgen Moltmann. English transl. copyright © 1983 by SCM Press Ltd. Reprinted by permission of HarperCollins Publishers.

26. Martin Luther, "A Father's Grief," from *The Theologia Germanica of Martin Luther*, transl. Bengt Hoffman. Mahwah, NJ: Paulist Press, 1980. Used by permission.

27. Peter Kreeft, "Shared Hells," from *Making Sense Out of Suffering*. Copyright © 1986 by Peter Kreeft. Published by Servant Publications, P.O. Box 8617, Ann Arbor, Michigan 48107. Used by permission.

28. Dag Hammarskjöld, "For the Sacrificed," from *Markings*, transl. W. H. Auden & Leif Sjoberg. Copyright © 1964, renewed 1992 by Alfred A. Knopf, a division of Random House

29. G. K. Chesterton, "God the Rebel," from *Orthodoxy*. New York: Dodd, Mead & Company, 1908.

30. Edith Stein, "Thy Will Be Done," from *Edith Stein: Essential Writings*, selected by John Sullivan, OCD. Maryknoll, New York: Orbis Books, 2002. Copyright © 2002 Washington Province of Discalced Carmelites, ISC Publications, 2131 Lincoln Road NE, Washington DC 20002.

31. Wendell Berry, "Still Bleeding," from *Jayber Crow*. Copyright © 2000 by Wendell Berry. Reprinted by permission of Counterpoint.

32. Dorothee Soelle, "On This Gallows," from *Suffering*, transl. Everett Kalin. Philadelphia, PA: Fortress Press, 1975. Copyright © 1975 by Fortress Press.

33. Henri Nouwen, "From Action to Passion," from *Finding My Way Home*, by Henri J. M. Nouwen. Chestnut Ridge, NY: Crossroad, 2004. Reprinted with permission from The Crossroad Publishing Company, Inc., www.crossroadpublishing.com.

34. Joseph Langford, "I Thirst for You," from *Mother Teresa's Secret Fire*, by Joseph Langford. Huntington, IN: Our Sunday Visitor, 2008. Copyright Missionaries of Charity Fathers. All rights reserved.

SECTION IV. CRUCIFIXION

Dylan Thomas, "This Bread I Break," from *The Poems of Dylan Thomas*. Copyright © 1943 by New Directions Publishing Corp. Reprinted by permission of New Directions Publishing Corp.

35. Saint Augustine, "Our Mediator," from *The Confessions*, transl. Maria Boulding. New York: Random House, 1998. Copyright © 1997 Augustinian Heritage Institute. Used by permission.

36. Thomas Howard, "The Crucifix," from *On Being Catholic*. San Francisco: Ignatius Press, 1997. Copyright © 1997 Ignatius Press.

37. Morton T. Kelsey, "The Cross and the Cellar," from *The Cross: Meditations on the Seven Last Words of Christ*. New York: Paulist Press, 1980. Copyright © 1980 by Morton T. Kelsey. Used by permission. www.paulistpress.com

38. Simone Weil, "The Distance," from *Waiting for God*, transl. Emma Craufurd. Translation copyright © 1951, renewed 1979 by G. P. Putnam's Sons. Used by permission of G. P. Putnam's Sons, a division of Penguin Group (USA) LLC; and from *Gravity and Grace*, transl. Arthur Wills. Translation copyright © 1947 by Libraire Plon. Used by permission of G. P. Putnam's Sons and Taylor & Francis Books UK.

39. John Stott, "Naked Pride," from *The Cross of Christ*. Copyright © 1986, 2006 by John R. W. Stott. Used by permission of InterVarsity Press, P.O. Box 1400, Downers Grove, IL 60515, www.ivpress.com, and Inter-Varsity Press, Nottingham, England.

40. Brennan Manning, "The Signature of Jesus," from *The Signature of Jesus*. Copyright © 1996 by Brennan Manning. Used by permission of WaterBrook Multnomah, an imprint of the Crown Publishing Group, a division of Random House LLC. All rights reserved.

41. Toyohiko Kagawa, "Life in the Blood," from *Meditations on the Cross*, transl. Helen F. Topping and Marion R. Draper. Copyright © 1935 by Willett, Clark & Company. Reprinted by permission of HarperCollins Publishers. Sadhu Sundar Singh, from *Wisdom of the Sadhu*, compiled and edited by Kim Comer (Plough, 2000).

42. Dale Aukerman, "The Central Murder," from "The Central Murder," in *Sojourners*, March 1980. Reprinted with permission from Sojourners, www.sojo.net.

43. Alexander Stuart Baillie, "Thirsting," from *The Seven Last Words*. St. Louis, MO: The Bethany Press, 1935.

44. Watchman Nee, "It Is Done," from *Sit, Walk, Stand*. Copyright © 1957 by Angus I. Kinnear. First published in 1957 by Gospel Literature Service, Bombay, India. American edition published in 1977 by Tyndale House Publishers, Inc., Wheaton, IL 60187. Used by permission of Tyndale House Publishers, Inc. All rights reserved.

45. George MacDonald, "The Father's Hands," from *The Unspoken Sermons*, originally published 1870–1891.

46. Paul Tillich, "A Cosmic Cross," from *The New Being*. Copyright © 1955 by Paul Tillich. New York: Charles Scribner's Sons, 1955.

SECTION V. RESURRECTION

John Updike, "Seven Stanzas at Easter," from *Telephone Poles and Other Poems*. Copyright © 1963 by John Updike. Used by permission of Alfred A. Knopf, an imprint of the Knopf Doubleday Publishing Group, a division of Random House LLC, and by permission of Penguin Books Ltd. All rights reserved.

47. C. S. Lewis, "The Strangest Story of All," from *God in the Dock*. Copyright © 1970 by C. S. Lewis Pte. Ltd. Reprinted by permission.

48. Frederica Mathewes-Green, "Merry Easter?" from "Easter Changes Everything," originally at www.beliefnet.com. Used by permission.

49. Alister E. McGrath, "In the Light of Victory," from *What Was God Doing on the Cross?*. Grand Rapids, MI: Zondervan Publishing House, 1992. Copyright © 1992 by Alister E. McGrath.

50. Howard Hageman, "Paradise Now," from *We Call This Friday Good*. Philadelphia, PA: Muhlenberg Press, 1961. Copyright © 1961 Muhlenburg Press.

51. Malcolm Muggeridge, "Impending Resurrection," from *Jesus: The Man Who Lives*. Copyright © 1975 by Malcolm Muggeridge. Reprinted by permission of HarperCollins Publishers.

52. Frederick Buechner, "The End Is Life," from *The Magnificent Defeat*. Copyright © 1966, 1994 by Frederick Buechner. Reprinted by permission of HarperCollins Publishers.

53. Dorothy Sayers, "The Greatest Drama," from *Spiritual Writings*, selected by Ann Loades. Boston, MA: Cowley Publications, 1993. Copyright © 1993 by Ann Loades.

54. Karl Barth, "Threatened by Resurrection," from *Come Holy Spirit: Sermons*, by Karl Barth and Eduard Thurneysen, transl. George Richards, Elmer G. Homrighausen, Karl Ernst. Eugene, OR: Wipf and Stock, 2010. Used by permission.

55. Walter J. Ciszek, "Fear Not," from *He Leadeth Me*, by Walter J. Ciszek with Daniel L. Flaherty. Copyright © 1973 by Walter J. Ciszek. Used by permission of Doubleday, an imprint of Knopf Doubleday Publishing Group, a division of Penguin Random House LLC. All rights reserved.

56. Madeleine L'Engle, "Waiting for Judas," from *The Rock That Is Higher*. Copyright © 1993, 2002 by Crosswicks. Used by permission of WaterBrook Multnomah, an imprint of the Crown Publishing Group, a division of Random House LLC. All rights reserved.

57. Dorothy Day, "The Mystery of the Poor," from *Dorothy Day: Selected Writings*, ed. by Robert Ellsberg. Maryknoll, NY: Orbis Books, 1983, 1992. Used by permission.

58. Philip Yancey, "Jesus' Reminders," from *Where Is God When It Hurts?*. Copyright © 1977, 1990 by Philip Yancey. Used by permission of Zondervan, www.zondervan.com.

SECTION VI. NEW LIFE

John Masefield, excerpted from "The Everlasting Mercy," in *The Poems and Plays of John Masefield*. New York: The Macmillan Company, 1924. Copyright © 1911 by John Masefield.

59. Leo Tolstoy, "I, Like the Thief," from *A Confession and What I Believe*, transl. Aylmer Maude. London: Oxford University Press, 1921.

60. Fyodor Dostoevsky, "Redemption," from *The Brothers Karamazov*, transl. Richard Pevear and Larissa Volokhonsky. Copyright © 1990 by Richard Pevear and Larissa Volokhonsky. Reprinted by permission of North Point Press, a division of Farrar, Straus and Giroux, LLC.

61. Alfred Kazin, "I Had Been Waiting," from *A Walker in the City*. Copyright © 1951, renewed 1979 by Alfred Kazin. Reprinted by permission of Houghton Mifflin Harcourt Publishing Company. All rights reserved.

62. E. Stanley Jones, "The Christ of Experience," from *The Christ of the Indian Road*. Copyright © 1925, renewed 1953 by Abingdon Press. Used by permission. All rights reserved.

63. Christoph Friedrich Blumhardt, "Christ Rising," from *Action in Waiting* (Plough, 1998); and from "Die and Jesus Will Live," an unpublished translation in the Bruderhof Archives, Walden, NY.

64. Amy Carmichael, "Calvary Love," from *If*. Copyright © 1938 by The Dohnavur Fellowship. Used by permission of CLC Publications. All rights reserved.

65. Johann Christoph Arnold, "The Power of Forgiveness," adapted from *Why Forgive?* (Plough, 2010).

66. Jürgen Moltmann, "The Feast of Freedom," from *The Power of the Powerless*. English transl. copyright © 1983 by SCM Press Ltd. Reprinted by permission of HarperCollins Publishers.

67. Clarence Jordan, "At God's Expense," from *The Substance of Faith and Other Cotton Patch Sermons*. New York: Association Press, 1972. Copyright © 1972 by Florence Jordan. Used by permission of Koinonia Partners, Inc.

68. Henri Nouwen, "Jesus Gives All," from *The Road to Daybreak*. Copyright © 1988 by Henri J. M. Nouwen. Used by permission of the Henri Nouwen Legacy Trust and of Doubleday, an imprint of the Knopf Doubleday Publishing Group, a division of Random House LLC. All rights reserved. (*The Road to Daybreak* is published in the USA by Penguin Random House and in the UK and Commonwealth by Darton, Longman and Todd); and from *Walk with Jesus: Stations of the Cross*. Maryknoll NY: Orbis Books, 1990, 2015. Used by permission.

69. Joyce Hollyday, "An Invitation," from "An Invitation to Faith" in *Sojourners*, April 1987. Reprinted with permission from Sojourners, www.sojo.net.

70. N. T. Wright, "A New World" from *The Crown and the Fire*. Copyright © 1992 by N. T. Wright. London: SPCK, 1992. Used by permission.

71. John Howard Yoder, "The Way of Peace," from *He Came Preaching Peace*. Scottdale, PA: Herald Press, 1985, 2004. Used by permission.

72. Eberhard Arnold, "Spirit of Fire," from *Innerland: A Guide into the Heart of the Gospel* (Plough, 1999); and from two unpublished talks (EAE 20/10, EAE 230) in the Bruderhof Archives, Walden, NY.

Index of Authors

If you liked
Bread and Wine
you should have
the companion volume…

WATCH FOR THE LIGHT

Readings for Advent and Christmas

THOUGH BELIEVERS the world over make yearly preparations for Lent, there's a conspicuous lack of good books for that other great spiritual season: Advent. All the same, this four-week period leading up to Christmas is making a comeback as growing numbers of people reject shopping mall frenzy.

WATCH FOR THE LIGHT contains daily Advent meditations from favorite classic and contemporary spiritual writers. Ecumenical in scope, these forty essays and poems celebrate the miracle of Christ's birth and infuse it with rich meaning for today. Includes writings by Thomas Aquinas, Dietrich Bonhoeffer, Dorothy Day, Annie Dillard, John Donne, Meister Eckhart, T. S. Eliot, Søren Kierkegaard, C. S. Lewis, Brennan Manning, Thomas Merton, Kathleen Norris, Henri Nouwen, Oscar Romero, Philip Yancey, and many others.

Related Titles from Plough

Discipleship: *Living for Christ in the Daily Grind*
J. Heinrich Arnold

*Sometimes sensitive, sometimes provocative, but always encouraging,
Arnold guides readers toward leading Christlike lives amid the stress
and strain of modern life.*

Provocations: *Spiritual Writings of Kierkegaard*
*Impassioned essays, parables, and sayings from the cantankerous Dane
whose writings pare away the fluff of modern spirituality to reveal the
essence of a Christ-centered life.*

Seeking Peace: *Notes & Conversations Along the Way*
Johann Christoph Arnold

*Everyone is seeking peace, but few seem to find it. Arnold points the
way through stories of ordinary people who have sought and found a
peace the world cannot give.*

Wisdom of the Sadhu: *Teachings of Sundar Singh*
*A famous Indian mystic who embraced faith in Christ but rejected
Christianity's western trappings gives the gospel new life in these
refreshing parables and meditations.*

Plough Publishing House
www.plough.com
*PO Box 398, Walden, NY 12586, USA
Robertsbridge, East Sussex TN32 5DR, UK
4188 Gwydir Highway, Elsmore, NSW 2360, AU*